Real Men Who Suffer Too

A Guide that Brings About Awareness of Male Victims and Domestic Violence

By Sheilah Y. Kimble

Dedication

To my daughter, Ardys S. Duncantell, my sons Marcus D. Perry and Arthur Lee Duncantell II (may he Rest in Paradise), my grandsons, as well as granddaughters, and to all males, known and unknown, who are victims of domestic violence, to my nephews, male cousins, uncles, and male friends. To those who are familiar with domestic violence and the consequences behind it.

Table of Contents

Chapter 1

Nothing but the Facts, Please!!!!

Society's attitudes are that women are perceived as being the typical victims or survivors of domestic violence. That are the facts. To further interject, society also assumes that most perpetrators are men. Fortunately, with books such as these and more research being conducted, these views are beginning to shape different stances on how society view and responds to those who are victims and survivors of domestic violence. It should be noted that since the early 1970s, the United States and several western societies such as New Zealand, the United Kingdom, and Australia do not just focus on women as being the victims of domestic violence; they also focus on men.

The facts are that domestic violence is a serious issue not only in the United States but around the world. Has anyone ever stopped to think that men can also be victims of domestic violence? Well, yes, this is true, and yes, men are also victims of domestic violence. It is not that domestic violence against women is not important, but it must also be recognized that domestic violence against men does exist and that it is just as equally important as domestic violence against women, and that all the violence must come to an end.

The facts are that as of 2017, there were at least 1 in 7 men and 1 in 4 women whom an intimate partner domestically abused. "Twenty-two percent of women and 7% of men report that an intimate partner has physically assaulted them in their lifetime. Among female victims of IPV, 4% reported having been threatened with a gun by an intimate partner, and 1% sustained firearm injuries in these assaults."[1]

There are those who ask, why doesn't a victim just get up and leave the abusive relationship? Well, that is often easier said than done. There are several reasons why victims do not want to end their relationships. There are those who truly love their abuser and just prefer that the abuse just cease. Other reasons for victims being reluctant to leave their relationships could be because they are financially or economically dependent upon their abuser; they have a genuine concern for their abuser; they also have a genuine concern for the well-being of the children that are involved and have witnessed the abuse and how it affects the child; it could be for religious, moral, or family pressure for the victim to make the relationship work; it could also be that the victim lacks the knowledge of resources (such as shelters); another reason would be because the victim may also have a strong belief that their abuser will eventually change; and then there are several of other real and valid reasons why the victim may feel that it is impossible to leave the abuser.[2]

There are those individuals who are just ignorant enough to believe that victims of domestic abuse enjoy being abused, but these individuals who make such assumptions do not take the time to think about the victim's situation because they have

[1] Tjaden P, Thoennes N. *Full Report of the Prevalence, Incidence, and Consequences of Intimate Partner Violence Against Women: Findings from the National Violence Against Women Survey.* Washington D.C.: U.S. Department of Justice; 2000.
[2] California Partnership to End Domestic Violence (2012). Cpedv.org.

not walked a mile in the victim's shoes. What one must understand is that no one wants to be hurt or become a victim of any type of violence, nor does an individual deserve to be abused. Victims of abuse frequently hear comments from their abuser such as "You deserved it,"[3] or from those who are on the outside looking in, "You must really like getting beat, or you would have left."[4] Such statements can often obscure a survivor's ability to think clearly, making them feel as though it is their fault for being abused and that they should take responsibility for the violence that is delved out towards them.

With the extreme change in times and people now becoming more open about their personal business, this demonstrates that, in some ways, the increased amount of domestic violence can be a distressing sign of the times. Domestic violence does not have the same meaning as it did before the 1990s when everyone viewed domestic violence as a hush-hush but serious issue that meant it was a husband beating his wife.

Today, domestic violence encompasses a variety of violence in the home, which includes intimate violence abuse, elder abuse which includes child-to-parent violence, and parent-to-child violence.[5] Facts are that society thinks that domestic abuse is a family problem and should be dealt with behind closed doors, which in actuality, it is not a family problem. Domestic abuse affects everyone because the emotional, psychological, and mental damage that has been sustained is carried outside the home and oftentimes affects the victim's everyday life. The consequences of domestic violence go far beyond that of the family dynamics, which makes it "an issue that everyone should be concerned about. Factors such as medical expenses, work absenteeism, lost

---

[3] California Partnership to End Domestic Violence (2012). Cpedv.org.
[4] California Partnership to End Domestic Violence (2012). Cpedv.org. [5] www.bangornews.com/cgi-bin/article.cfm?storynumber=23006

wages, court costs, pain, suffering, and poor quality of life make domestic violence a significant social problem for everyone."[5]

The truth of the matter is that when an abuser decides to abuse their victim, it is because they choose to do so. The abusers' violent behavior is a choice that they make, not something that was forced upon them. "Perpetrators use violence to control their victims. Domestic violence is about batterers having and exerting absolute control, not losing control. Their actions are calculated and deliberate."[6] Society's attitude is that domestic violence isn't that serious. It is usually only a punch, push, shoves, slap, or what they may assume is something that is innocently meaningless. What society does not realize is that when such instances happen, oftentimes, it escalates. The abusive relationship can "result in serious injuries which require medical attention. Abusive incidents also can result in death."[7]

Society often assumes that victims of domestic violence provoke their abuser causing the abuser to lash out. The victim does not provoke the abuser to abuse them. The fact of the matter is that a victim who is being domestically abused can usually sense when the tension is beginning to escalate and that a beating is most likely to be imminent. "Victims often report that the period of tension preceding an abusive incident is much worse than that of the actual physical abuse. As a result, they may start a fight with their abuser in order to "get it over with" and end the unendurable tension. This behavior should not be considered provoking."[8]

---

[5] California Partnership to End Domestic Violence (2012). Cpedv.org.
[6] California Partnership to End Domestic Violence (2012). Cpedv.org.
[7] California Partnership to End Domestic Violence (2012). Cpedv.org.
[8] California Partnership to End Domestic Violence (2012). Cpedv.org.

What exactly is domestic violence? "Domestic violence is a range of behaviors that is used to establish power and exert control by one intimate partner over the other."[9] "Domestic violence is a pattern of assaultive and coercive behaviors that adults or adolescents use against their current or former intimate partners."[10] An abusive behavior is a pattern that has been learned, and such abuse is not an isolated incident. Society's attitudes are that "domestic violence is a one-time event or that it is an isolated incident or a momentary loss of temper. Again, the truth is that domestic violence is a common problem in the United States, as well as globally."[11] Generally, once the behavior begins in a relationship, it becomes increasingly violent and frequent over a period of time."[12] Don't believe the hype.

What many do not understand, especially if they have not been exposed to domestic violence or do not know anyone who is a victim of domestic violence, is that domestic violence is a learned behavior and that such violent behaviors are not caused by genetics. Abusive behaviors are choices that the abuser makes, and it is not caused by man-made chemicals such as drugs or alcohol, nor is it influenced by institutional and social responses. There is a common factor concerning domestic violence, and that is the fact that domestic violence is found in every culture, race, and socioeconomic class and is not immune to anyone. Many people in our society feel as though alcohol and drugs are contributing factors for domestic violence. The truth is that substance abuse is used as an excuse by the abuser for conducting the abusive behavior. Batterers who abuse their partners while under the influence of drugs or alcohol are also likely to do so while

[9] California Partnership to End Domestic Violence (2012). Cpedv.org.
[10] Missouri Coalition Against Domestic Violence.
[11] California Partnership to End Domestic Violence (2012). Cpedv.org.
[12] California Partnership to End Domestic Violence (2012). Cpedv.org.

sober.[13],[14] This statement has been repeated, but it is important to know that domestic violence is a serious matter globally.

Societal attitudes are that domestic violence only occurs among those who are economically impoverished or to those individuals of color.[15] This, too, is inaccurate. The truth is that "domestic violence occurs in families of all social, ethnic, racial, educational, and religious backgrounds. It occurs in towns, suburbs, rural areas, and cities. The frequency and severity of violence among people in a lower socio-economic class equals the frequency and severity amount in higher socio-economic classes. Victims in lower socio-economic classes may be more visible in society, as they often have a greater need for shelter services due to a lack of resources."[16]

What is abuse according to California's laws? Domestic abuse, according to the law in the State of California, is found under the California Penal Code 13700(a), which is defined as "Abuse" as intentionally or recklessly causing or attempting to cause bodily injury or placing another person in reasonable apprehension of imminent serious bodily injury to himself, herself or another. **Intimate partner violence** refers to behavior by an intimate partner or ex-partner that causes physical, sexual, or psychological harm, including physical aggression, sexual coercion, psychological abuse, and controlling behaviors.[17]

First, let's talk about dating abuse. Dating violence is a type of Intimate Partner Violence (IPV). It occurs between two people who are in a close relationship. The nature

---

[13] California Partnership to End Domestic Violence (2012). Cpedv.org.
[14] Source: Alcoholism: Clinical and Experimental Research
www.intelihealth.com/IH/ihtIH/WSIHW000/9105/342/348649.html
[15] California Partnership to End Domestic Violence (2012). Cpedv.org.
[16] California Partnership to End Domestic Violence (2012). Cpedv.org.
[17] (WHO Fact Sheet N°239, 2014)

of dating violence can be physical, emotional, psychological, economic, stalking, cyberbullying or technological, isolation, sexual and legal abuse. Physical violence occurs when a partner is pinched, pushed, choked, hit, shoved, slapped, punched, kicked, has food withheld, withholding a victim's medication or their access to mobility or sensory-related equipment, keeping a victim from seeking necessary medical attention, and other acts that inhibits a victim's physical well-being.

Psychological/Emotional—This means threatening a partner or harming his or her sense of self-worth. Examples include name-calling, shaming, bullying, embarrassing on purpose, lying, or making false allegations against them so that you can have a sense of control over them or keeping him/her away from friends and family. This also includes other acts that seek to lower a victim's self-esteem.[18]

Sexual—This is forcing a partner to engage in a sex act when he or she does not or cannot consent. This can be physical or nonphysical, like threatening to spread rumors if a partner refuses to have sex, forcing them to watch porn, and so forth. Stalking—This refers to using a pattern of harassing or threatening tactics that are unwanted and causes fear in the victim.[19]

Domestic abuse that many do not think about or consider to be abuse is cyberbullying or technological abuse, which is also a sign of abuse. This includes the misuse of technology (like mobile devices, computers, GPS, and social media) to stalk, harass and exert power and control over a victim.[20]

---

[18] California Partnership to End Domestic Violence (2012). Cpedv.org.
[19] California Partnership to End Domestic Violence (2012). Cpedv.org.
[20] California Partnership to End Domestic Violence (2012). Cpedv.org.
[22] © 2018 New York State Coalition Against Domestic Violence

Economic abuse is controlling the money, bank accounts, or assets belonging to the family; not allowing the victim to work; interfering with the victim's work to the point that they lose their job; making the victim completely responsible for bringing in income to the family; and other acts that set up a financial dependence in the relationship.[22]

Isolation can include preventing a victim's contact with family and friends, relocating a victim to a new location where they don't know anyone, controlling a victim's interactions with people, and other acts that separate a victim from their support network.[21]

Stalking can include repeated and unnecessary contact via text message, phone calls, email, or social media, planned appearances at places that the victim frequents, monitoring the victim's activities through the use of technology, and other acts that control a victim's movement or induce fear.[22]

Legal abuse is threatening to or divorcing of the victim, the threatening to or taking all assets, threatening to or taking custody of children or pets, taking away all identifying documents (ex., Marriage license, passports, ID cards, etc.), the promising to help the partner to file for status but never doing it the threatening to report immigration status to ICE.[23]

The society also says that "Stress (such as financial difficulty or problems at work) causes abuse. Once the stressful situation is resolved, the abuse will stop."[24] The

---

[21] © 2018 New York State Coalition Against Domestic Violence

[22] © 2018 New York State Coalition Against Domestic Violence

[23] California Partnership to End Domestic Violence (2012). Cpedv.org.

[24] California Partnership to End Domestic Violence (2012). Cpedv.org.

[27] California Partnership to End Domestic Violence (2012). Cpedv.org.

truth is, "Abuse is not caused by stress. Some abusers may experience stress, but stress does not cause abusive behaviors. Abusers may use stress as an excuse for their behavior, but even after the stress is reduced, the abuse can continue."[27]

Some of the signs of domestic violence can be that the abuser may begin behaving in an over-protective manner or may be extremely jealous. The abuser will suddenly become angry or lose their temper, become possessive, and they will begin to destroy the victim's personal property or throw things around, or may even begin throwing items at the victim. The abuser will even go so far as to control how the victim dresses. The abuser will consistently threaten to do harm to the victim, their children, pets, family members, friends, or even themselves. The abuser may constantly call, text, or email the victim at an excessive rate trying to pinpoint exactly where the victim is at.

The abuser may also want the victim to facetime them so that they can tell whether or not the victim is being truthful. This will also allow the abuser to be able to see the victim through the video chat, which will display exactly where the victim is at and who the victim is with. The abuser will usually deny the victim access to resources, such as bank accounts, credit cards, or the car. The abuser will even go as far as to control all of the victim's finances and force the victim to account for what and where they spend their money. The abuser may go to the victim's place of employment and create problems that can cause the victim to be terminated. Many times, the abuser will even go as far as to file false police reports against the victim, twisting the situation and having the victim arrested under false pretenses or hacking the victim's phone or computer and posting negative images to make it seem as though the victim is the actual abuser and taking the focus from the actual abuser.

If the abuser is in the military, they may exploit their military status to prevent the victim from leaving. In other instances, if the victim is trying to better their situation by going back to school or trying to obtain or maintain better employment, the abuser will try and prevent the victim from completing their schoolwork or work tasks. The abuser will either limit or prevent the victim from seeing family or friends. They will control where the victim can go, when they can go, and who they are with. The abuser will even use the victim's status within a religious community to harass, threaten, or intimidate them. The abuser will make the victim participate in behaviors that will make the victim question their mental health. The abuser will also threaten to expose the victim's citizenship status or have the victim deported, deny the victim access to their immigration documents, and use intimidation or manipulation to control the victim or the victim's children. There are even times when the abuser will go as far as making the victim perform certain acts or even sexual acts that the victim does not want to perform.

The abuser will control the victim's expression of gender identity or sexual orientation or even threaten to "out" the victim if the victim is lesbian, gay, bisexual, transgender, or queer.[25]

In keeping all of this in mind, remember that each state has different laws concerning domestic violence. The State of New York, for instance, has the following laws. Assault crimes including Third Degree Assault (NY PL 120.00) & Second Degree Assault (NY PL 120.05) : Examples include punches and kicks that cause "substantial pain" such as redness and bruising. Felony examples may include the use of a

---

[25] © 2018 New York State Coalition Against Domestic Violence

"dangerous instrument" or the causing of a more serious physical injury such as one that leaves an ugly scar. <u>Aggravated Harassment</u> in the Second Degree (NY PL 240.30) : Examples of <u>Second Degree Aggravated Harassment</u> include repeated phone calls or texts that serve no legitimate purpose or merely harass the other party. <u>Aggravated Criminal Contempt</u> (NY PL 215.52) and <u>Criminal Contempt</u> (NY PL 215.51 and NY PL 215.50): Examples include violating orders of protection or restraining orders without or without threats or physical injuries.

    <u>Stalking in the Fourth Degree</u> (NY PL 120.45), <u>Stalking in the Third Degree</u> (NY PL 120.50) and <u>Stalking in the Second Degree</u> (NY PL 120.55): An example may include following a person to work or around the neighborhood while putting that person in fear for their safety. Weapons enhance this crime. **Menacing in the Third Degree** (NY PL 120.15) and **Menacing in the Second Degree** (NY PL 120.14): Examples include threatening to hurt another person with or without some form of weapon or dangerous instrument. <u>Strangulation and Related Offenses</u> including <u>Obstruction of Breathing or Blood Circulation</u> (NY PL 121.11) and <u>Strangulation in the Second Degree</u> (NY PL 121.12): A common accusation of prosecutors; an example may occur when you put your hands on another party's neck and squeeze even slightly. <u>Endangering the Welfare of a Child</u> (NY PL 260.10): Examples of **Endangering the Welfare of a Child** may include striking a child, Assault of another in front of that child, or using drugs around a child.

    <u>Criminal Mischief crimes</u> including **Criminal Mischief in the Fourth Degree** (NY PL 145.00) & **Criminal Mischief in the Third Degree** (NY PL 145.05): Examples may include breaking a cell or mobile phone, damaging furniture or scratching a car.

The dollar amount of the damage dictates the level of the crime. <u>Robbery in the Third</u> <u>Degree</u> (NY PL 160.05) & <u>Grand Larceny Fourth Degree</u> (NY PL 155.30(5)) : An example can include taking a cell phone from another person's hand. If force is used, the felony goes from **Fourth Degree Grand Larceny to Third Degree Robbery**.

<u>Computer crimes</u> including <u>Unauthorized Use of a Computer,</u> (NY PL 156.05), <u>Computer Trespass</u> (NY PL 156.10) : Examples may include accessing emails or texts of a partner or family member. Other examples could be altering passwords or sending out bogus emails from another person's account.[26]

In the State of Illinois, domestic battery is a Class A misdemeanor charge under Illinois law. The possible sentence for any Class A misdemeanor in Illinois is up to one year in jail and a fine of $2,500[27]. The statute provides the following: Section *12-3.2.*

Domestic Battery.

(a) A person commits domestic battery if he intentionally or knowingly without legal justification by any means:

1) Causes bodily harm to any family or household member as defined in subsection (3) of Section 112A-3 of the Code of Criminal Procedure of 1963, as amended.

2) Makes physical contact of an insulting or provoking nature with any family or household member as defined in subsection (3) of Section 112A-3 of the Code of Criminal Procedure of 1963, as amended.[28]

Illinois states that in a Domestic Relationship all the prosecution basically needs to do is to prove two things in a domestic violence case: first, a battery, and second, a

---

[26] © 1996-2018 - New York State Office of Court Administration - All Rights Reserved. (<u>Title 17 U.S.C.</u>)

[27] **www.illinoisattorneygeneral.gov**/women/victims.html

[28] **www.chicagonow.com**/blogs/**criminal-lawyer-illinois**/2010/08/what-is-the-laws-on-domestic-violence

domestic relationship. Anyone who is a family or household member falls into the category of a domestic relationship, the law says: "Family or household members include spouses, former spouses, parents, children, stepchildren, and other persons related by blood or by present or prior marriage, persons who share or formerly shared a common dwelling, persons who have or allegedly have a child in common, persons who shar or allegedly share a blood relationship through a child, persons who have or have had a dating or engagement relationship, persons with disabilities and their personal assistants, and caregivers as defined in paragraph (3) of subsection (b) of Section 12-21 of the Criminal Code of 1961. See 750 ILCS 60/103(6).[29]

In the state of Illinois some of the laws concerning domestic violence are the increased reports of strangulation which has become very serious, which is becoming the leading cause of death in many of the domestic violence deaths. It is only in recent years that the State of Illinois has recognized that strangulation "has been identified as of one of the most lethal forms of domestic violence.[30]" "As a result, more than half of the states, in this country, have passed criminal laws specifically dealing with strangulation."[31] On the 1st of January 2010, the State of Illinois' "first strangulation statutes went into effect."[32] What is the definition of "Strangulation" it is intentionally impeding the normal breathing or circulation of the blood of an individual by applying

[29] www.**chicagonow.com**/blogs/**criminal-law**yer-**illinois**/2010/08/what-is-the-laws-on-domestic-violence

[30] Content for the Domestic Violence Newsletter which is provided by the Chicago Police Department's Domestic Violence Program., 3510 South Michigan Avenue, 3rd Floor, Chicago, Illinois,60653• Phone:(312)745-6340• Fax (312)745-6856 FEBRUARY 2010

[31] Content for the Domestic Violence Newsletter which is provided by the Chicago Police Department's Domestic Violence Program., 3510 South Michigan Avenue, 3rd Floor, Chicago, Illinois,60653• Phone:(312)745-6340• Fax (312)745-6856 FEBRUARY 2010

[32] Content for the Domestic Violence Newsletter which is provided by the Chicago Police Department's Domestic Violence Program., 3510 South Michigan Avenue, 3rd Floor, Chicago, Illinois,60653• Phone:(312)745-6340• Fax (312)745-6856 FEBRUARY 2010

pressure on the throat or neck of that individual or by blocking the nose or mouth of that individual. In the State of Illinois Aggravated Domestic Battery is a simple battery against a family or household member that is committed by strangulation, which will be charged as Aggravated Domestic Battery-720 ILCS 5/12-3.3 (a) (5). Aggravated Domestic Battery is a Class 2 felony.[33] "ILLINOIS' NEW STRANGULATION LAW Illinois has amended the Aggravated Battery and Aggravated Domestic Battery statutes to allow what would otherwise be a misdemeanor battery to be charged as a felony."[34]

Aggravated Battery according to the laws in Illinois is a "person who commits a battery against another person by strangulation may be charged with Aggravated Battery, 720 ILCS 5/12-4. Aggravated Battery is typically a Class 3 felony, carrying a penalty of 2-5 years. The sentence can be enhanced for Aggravated Battery by strangulation to a Class 1 felony, carrying a penalty of not less than 4 years and up to 15 years, if any of the following conditions apply: domestic violence related. Many of those victims died without a single visible mark to their neck.[35]

Some of the laws concerning domestic violence in the State of Tennessee are those such as the Penalties for Breaking Tennessee's Domestic Violence Laws. Penalties include losing your right to possess firearms if you're convicted of domestic assault or someone obtains a protection order against you. If a person is found to have a gun after a domestic violence conviction or while a protection order is in place, it's considered a

---

[33] Nancy Glass, Kathy Laughon, Jacquelyn Campbell, Anne D. Wolf Chair, Carolyn Rebecca Block, Ginger Hanson, Phyllis W. Sharps, Ellen Taliaferro, Non-fatal strangulation is an important risk factor for homicide of women, J. Emerg Med, Vol. 35, No.3 (2008)

[34] Content for the Domestic Violence Newsletter which is provided by the Chicago Police Department's Domestic Violence Program., 3510 South Michigan Avenue, 3rd Floor, Chicago, Illinois,60653• Phone:(312)745-6340• Fax (312)745-6856 FEBRUARY 2010

[35] Gael B. Strack, George E. McClane, Dean Hawley, A Review of 300 Attempted Strangulation Cases (Part 1: Criminal Legal Issues, Part 2: Clinical Evaluation of the Surviving Victim, Part 3: Injuries in Fatal Cases); J Emerg Med, Vol.21, No.3 (2001).

Class A misdemeanor and each violation is a separate offense (meaning multiple sentences can be imposed). In addition, a fine of up to $200 will be imposed based on the defendant's ability to pay. This fine goes to the Tennessee general fund for family violence shelters and services.[36]

****Victim Resources and Protection Orders****

If you're a survivor of domestic violence in Tennessee and haven't yet reached out for help, please try contacting the Tennessee Coalition to End Domestic & Sexual Violence. If you don't yet have a protection order, it may be a good idea to obtain one. You may want to seek the help of a domestic violence lawyer. Having a protection order will allow you to call the police and have your abuser arrested if he or she comes after you in violation of the protection order.[37] 2010 Tennessee Code Title 39 - Criminal Offenses Chapter 13 - Offenses Against Person Part 1 - Assaultive Offenses 39-13-111 - Domestic assault.

(a)   As used in this section, domestic abuse victim means any person who falls within the following categories:

(1)   Adults or minors who are current or former spouses.

(2)   Adults or minors who live together or who have lived together.

---

[36] Copyright © 2018, Thomson Reuters. All rights reserved. Also, from Tennessee Statutes Relating to Domestic Violence, Assault, Stalking, and Sex Offenses," and "The Tennessee Code is provided online by Lexis Law Publishing at: http://198.187.128.12/tennessee/lpext.dll?f=templates&fn=fs-main.htm&2.0
[37] Tennessee Statutes Relating to Domestic Violence, Assault, Stalking, and Sex Offenses," and "The Tennessee Code is provided online by Lexis Law Publishing at: http://198.187.128.12/tennessee/lpext.dll?f=templates&fn=fsmain.htm&2.0

(3)   Adults or minors who are dating or who have dated or who have or had a sexual relationship, but does not include fraternization between two (2) individuals in a business or social context.

(4)   Adults or minors related by blood or adoption.

(5)   Adults or minors who are related or were formerly related by marriage; or

(6)   Adult or minor children of a person in a relationship that is described in subdivisions (a)(1)-(5).

(b)   A person commits domestic assault who commits an assault as defined in § 39-13-

101 against a domestic abuse victim.

(c)(1) Domestic assault is punishable the same as assault in § 39-13-101.

(2)   In addition to any other punishment that may be imposed for a violation of this section, if, as determined by the court, the defendant possesses the ability to pay a fine in an amount not in excess of two hundred dollars ($200), then the court shall impose a fine at the level of the defendant's ability to pay, but not in excess of two hundred dollars ($200). The additional fine shall be paid to the clerk of the court imposing sentence, who shall transfer it to the state treasurer, who shall credit the fine to the general fund. All fines so credited to the general fund shall be subject to appropriation by the general assembly for the exclusive purpose of funding family violence shelters and shelter services. This appropriation shall be in addition to any amount appropriated pursuant to § 67-4-411.

(3)   A person convicted of a violation of this section shall be required to terminate, upon conviction, possession of all firearms that the person possesses as required by § 36-3-625. [Acts 2000, Ch. 824, § 1; 2002, Ch. 649, § 3; 2008, Ch. 744, § 1; 2009, Ch.

455, § 4.][38]

In the State of Georgia, the laws concerning domestic violence, is an act of "family violence." The law protects against physical, sexual, and emotional abuse among family members. You don't have to be married to someone in order to be a victim of domestic violence in Georgia. 2010 In the State of Georgia, the laws concerning domestic violence, is an act of "family violence." The law protects against physical, sexual, and emotional abuse among family members.

You don't have to be married to someone in order to be a victim of domestic violence in Georgia. 2010 Georgia Code Title 19-Domestic Relations Chapter 13-Family Violence-Article 1-Granting of Relief by Superior Courts § 19-13-1 - "Family violence" defined O.C.G.A. 19-13-1 (2010) 19-13-1. "Family violence" is defined as used in this article, the term "family violence" means the occurrence of one or more of the following acts between past or present spouses, persons who are parents of the same child, parents and children, stepparents and stepchildren, foster parents and foster children, or other persons living or formerly living in the same household: (1) Any felony; or (2) Commission of offenses of battery, simple battery, simple assault, assault, stalking, criminal damage to property, unlawful restraint, or criminal trespass. The term "family violence" shall not be deemed to include reasonable discipline administered by a parent to a child in the form of corporal punishment, restraint, or detention.

Of course, the law for each state is different, however this is just an example of what each state has enacted concerning domestic violence. "Everyone quotes the statistics given by the National Coalition Against Domestic Violence: 1 in 4 women will

---

[38] law.justia.com

be victims of domestic violence at some point in their lives, 1.3 million women are assaulted by their partner every year, 85% of domestic violence reported is against women. However, in a conflicting survey taken by the CDC in 2010, it was found that 40% of the victims of severe, physical domestic violence were men. Despite the many findings that shows almost equal amounts of abuse perpetuated against men and women, the media and government focus their attention mostly on the female victims of domestic violence. Men are largely silent on the issue because of the perception that men are physically stronger and should be able to subdue a female attacker easily. Those men who do report physical violence are more likely to be ridiculed—by law enforcement, the judicial system and by the public—than women are."[39]

Fatalities against men who are victims in domestic violent relationships are rapidly increasing. Oftentimes their abusers are jealous wives, girlfriends, or ex's. The sad part is that there is very little research that has been done concerning the statistical facts of domestic abuse against men. There are many agencies including the Justice Department who focuses their attention more on women who are victims of domestic violence, instead of male victims of domestic violence; so, they will limit funding if provide any funding at all towards research. And because there is a lack of funding to do adequate research, there are those individuals who are able to perpetuate such myths concerning men and women who are victims of domestic violence. Some myths are that women are only violent when defending themselves, or that men could more easily leave a violent relationship than a woman can. Again, because of lack of funding, there are also few shelters that cater to men. Many of the shelters that are available will only take

[39] Ruth, S. "Men: The Overlooked Victims of Domestic Violence." May 16, 2012. *Figure taken from Men Web: CDC/DOJ Survey Men more often victims of intimate partner violence. http://www.batteredmen.com/NISVS.htm*

women and children, and even with that being said, some of these shelters even have an age limit on the boys that they will take in (13 years old)."[40]

In 1993, there was a made for television movie titled, "Men Don't Tell" based on the screenplay written by Jeff Andrus who passed away in 2011. This movie starred Peter Strauss and Judith Light. The movie, which was based on a true story, that was about a loving husband who for years was terrorized by his wife's violent behavior. In the movie, Strauss's daughter breaks her silence and reveals to her retired police officer, paternal grandfather that her mommy hits her daddy as her father, the retired police officer's son is being interrogated by the police at the station and her mommy lays in the hospital.

A book I am working on I titled "Real Men Don't Tell," (information in this book and the title was copywritten 2013 but cannot be completed until my son's murder investigation is completed. Currently his murder is not being investigated due to institutional racism and it has been 7 years, but I will leave that at that for obvious reasons). The reason why I chose this title is because I remember the movie "Men Don't Tell" being ridiculed by several women's groups because men are supposed to exemplify the character of a robust male, as one with strength and not weakness, one who takes charge of a situation and navigates himself through the pitfalls of life, especially if you are living an urban life or in areas that are economically impoverished. There are so many hurdles that men must overcome in life and in dealing with such hurdles it is a lot to take in.

---

[40] S. Ruth, "Men: The Overlooked Victims of Domestic Violence." May 16, 2012. *Figure taken from Men Web: CDC/DOJ Survey Men more often victims of intimate partner violence. http://www.batteredmen.com/NISVS.htm*

In my upcoming book "Real Men Don't Tell" it is about males who are victims of domestic violence from all walks of life. Many are those whom I know personally and took the time to share their story with me. They are boys, teenagers, young adults, old men, Black men, White men, Asian men, Latin men, and Native American men, they are rich, and they are poor. Real men of domestic violence are different ethnicities, backgrounds, religions and races. It is often wondered, why isn't there ever a public outpouring of grief concerning men who are killed as a result of domestic violence? Why is it that men who are abused are not taken as serious? Domestic violence against men does exits. It may not exist in the sense that it is more traditionally common among women than men, but it does exits. Instead of turning a blind eye and ignoring that there are men who are also victims of domestic violence, we must come up with solutions to solve the problem at hand concerning both men and women who are victims of domestic violence instead of using smoke and mirrors as though these instances does not exist. We must come up with those answers that will answer our questions, and explanations that will explain how those solutions will be affective not just for women, but for men as well.

Philip W. Cook was an American journalist and the author of "Abused Men—The Hidden Side of Domestic Violence. He did extensive research about why domestic abuse against men is so underreported. He is quoted as saying, "It is often said that some things are just not supposed to happen that way, but oftentimes it does, and it usually happens more often than one may think. When the situation presents itself, it is at one point or another in your lifetime, and it may happen to you, what will you do?"[41]

---

[41] *Cook, Phillip W.* (1997). *Abused Men: The Hidden Side of Domestic Violence.* Westport, CT: Praeger. pp. 43–91. *ISBN 9780313356711.*

Whether you are black, white, red, yellow or brown, rich or poor, stop and think about it from an analytical point of view. In Cook's book he states that "the first comprehensive survey based on a general nationally representative sample was originally made available to the public in 1977 and then published in book form in 1980. *Behind Closed Doors: Violence In the American Family,"* by Murray Straus, Richard Gelles, and Suzanne Steinmetz.[42]

Many in mainstream society only hears half the truth about domestic violence against males by females because they always make the stereotypical assumption that females are always the victims and males are always the perpetrators. However, there is another side to this story which is a side that simply does not get told or as stated earlier, many refuse to believe that such violence exists. The reason why this side of the story does not get told is because domestic violence against men has been "systematically ignored and marginalized because people think that domestic violence against men simply do not exist due to advocates and the media only telling half the truth."[43]

While society focuses the majority of their attention on female victims of domestic violence, they forget that there is little to nothing being done to protect men who are victims of domestic violence. Additionally, has anyone ever stopped to think that domestic violence against men is wrong? There are also men who are falsely accused of being abusers, but then that issue falls under a different category. Society

---

[42] *Cook, Phillip W.* (1997). *Abused Men: The Hidden Side of Domestic Violence.* Westport, CT: Praeger. pp. 43–91. *ISBN 9780313356711.*
[43] http://batteredmen.com/Journal.htm

must understand that domestic violence is no longer exclusive to being a male on female issue, it now goes both ways.

Chapter 2

Hurt, Harm and Homicide

Studies show that in 2007, there were more than 18,000 homicides in the U.S.[44] "While men are more likely to be homicide victims, women are over 3 and a half times more likely to be killed by an intimate partner compared to men."[45] According to federal data that was collected from police departments, in 2005 there were approximately 40% of female homicide victims that were between the ages of 15–50 who were killed by either a current or former intimate partner.[49] In over half (55%) of these cases, the perpetrator used a gun. That same data further revealed that among male victims who were between the ages of 15–50, there were 2% of males who were killed by either a current or former intimate partner. About 37% of the male intimate partner homicides also involved a gun.[50] A 2014 study conducted by Every town for Gun Safety reported

[44] Centers for Disease Control and Prevention. Web-based Injury Statistics Query and Reporting System (WISQARS) [Online]. (2007). National Center for Injury Prevention and Control, Centers for Disease Control and Prevention (producer). Available from: URL: www.cdc.gov/ncipc/wisqars. [2010 Sep 16].

[45] Fox JA, Zawitz MW. *Homicide Trends in the United States.* Washington, D.C.: Bureau of Justice Statistics; 2006.

[49] Fox JA, Zawitz MW. *Homicide Trends in the United States.* Washington, D.C.: Bureau of Justice Statistics; 2006.

[50] Fox JA, Zawitz MW. *Homicide Trends in the United States.* Washington, D.C.: Bureau of Justice Statistics; 2006.

that 59 percent of 100-plus mass shootings (four or more people killed) between January 2009 and June 2014 involved the murder of an intimate partner or family member.

When it comes to hurt, harm and homicide, domestic violence again is a serious issue. Emotional and psychological abuse is part of the hurt, harm, and homicide. This type of abuse is aimed towards chipping away at one's feelings of self-worth as well as their independence. Males are very much so victims of emotional abuse, and the harm is that most males may feel that trying to get out of an abusive relationship is virtually impossible or that if they leave their abusive partner then they would be left with nothing. For the male, the emotional abuse will be verbal abuse, yelling, belittling, name-calling, blaming, and shaming. Other forms of emotional abuse is isolation, intimidation, and using a controlling behavior which also falls under emotional abuse. Furthermore, those abusers who use emotional and/or psychological abuse usually throws in threats of physical violence in order to have a tighter hold and control over their victim.

There are those who may think that the physical abuse that is done towards a victim is far worse than emotional abuse, but that is not completely true. Physical violence can send an individual to the hospital leaving them with scars. Physical violence can also kill an individual. Whichever the case, emotional abuse and the scars from the effects of it are very real, and they can run deep. The facts are that emotional abuse can be just as damaging as physical abuse, oftentimes even more so. Furthermore, the end results of emotional abuse will usually worsen over time, often escalating to the physical abuse.

It seems that domestic violence gained written recognition in 1974 when Erin

Pizzey published her book *"Scream Quietly or Neighbors Will Hear,"* where she is "generally credited with starting the modem of the women's movement against domestic violence."[46] Between 1980 to 2008 it seems that all of the homicide victims were females which accounted for (41.5%). Female victims were almost 6 times more likely than male murder victims (7.1%) to have been killed by an intimate partner."[47] Take notice, there were still 7.1% of males that were victims of homicide, killed by an intimate partner. In "an analysis of statistics on domestic violence, it shows the number of men who were attacked by their wives, girlfriends or ex's which is much higher than many may think. A report in, *Domestic Violence: The Male Perspective*, stated, 'Domestic violence is often seen as the female being the victim and the male being the perpetrator problem, but as evidence is looked at more closely, it demonstrates that such accuracies paint a false picture of such issues.[53]

According to the ONS statistics for 20011-2012 studies show that while 1.2 million women experienced domestic violence, they also show that more than 800,000 men also experienced some form of domestic violence.[48] In 1994 a veteran criminal lawyer by the name of Alan Dershowitz wrote a paper while at the University of Iowa that reported over 40% of U.S. spousal murders were perpetrated by women.[49] Men who are assaulted by their female partners are usually ignored by law enforcement, the

---

[46] Cook, Phillip W. (1997). *Abused Men: The Hidden Side of Domestic Violence*. Westport, CT: Praeger. pp. 43–91. *ISBN 9780313356711.*
[47] Homicide trends in the US 1980-2008, cooper smith. http://www.bjs.gov/content/pub/pdf/htus8008.pdf [53] Campbell, Denis (September 5, 2010*). "More than 40% of domestic violence victims are male, report reveals". The Guardian.*
[48] Woolfe, N. Quentin. "Our attitude to violence against men is out of date." Written on April 9, 2014. © Copyright of Telegraph Media Group Limited 2018
[49] Woolfe, N. Quentin. "Our attitude to violence against men is out of date." Written on April 9, 2014. © Copyright of Telegraph Media Group Limited 2018

judicial system and the media which allows their perpetrator to go free. Unfortunately, for the male victim, there is very limited to no resources that are available for them to seek refuge.

Even in Great Britain, the data from their "Home Office statistical bulletins and the British Crime Survey shows that men made up about 40% of domestic violence victims each year between 2004-05 and 2008-09, with the last year for which figures are available. In 2006-07 men made up 43.4% of all those who had suffered partner abuse in the previous year, which rose to 45.5% in 2007-08 but fell to 37.7% in 200809. This is similar to the statistic in the United States."[50] There are those who "claim that men are often treated as 'second-class victims' and that many police forces and councils do not take male victims of domestic violence seriously."[51] This is one reason why male victims of domestic violence goes unnoticed or are virtually invisible to the "authorities such as the police, who rarely can be prevailed upon to take the man's side,"[52] said John Mays of Parity. "Their plight is largely overlooked by the media, official reports or in government policy. For example, some reports showed that in the provision of refuge places, the numbers showed 7,500 for females in England and Wales but only 60 for men."[53]

We must keep in mind that both women and men can be victims of domestic violence, in addition society must understand that "the number of women prosecuted

---

[50] Campbell, Denis (September 5, 2010). *"More than 40% of domestic violence victims are male, report reveals"*. *The Guardian.*
[51] Campbell, Denis (September 5, 2010). *"More than 40% of domestic violence victims are male, report reveals"*. *The Guardian.*
[52] Campbell, Denis (September 5, 2010). *"More than 40% of domestic violence victims are male, report reveals"*. *The Guardian.*
[53] Campbell, Denis (September 5, 2010). *"More than 40% of domestic violence victims are male, report reveals"*. *The Guardian..*

for domestic violence rose from 1,575 in 2004-05 to 4,266 in 2008-09."[54] Some of the hurt and harm that men develop being victims of domestic violence is "psychological aggression and control over sexual or reproductive health. Another aspect of psychological abuse that men have experienced is 48.8% with at least one male experiencing a form of psychologically aggressive behavior such as the abuser keeping track and demanding to know his whereabouts, being insulted or humiliated in front of family, friends, coworkers, and even strangers or being threatened by their intimate partner's actions in their lifetime.[55] With that being said, there are 4 in 10 men who have experienced at least some form of intimidating control (isolation from friends and family, manipulation, blackmail, deprivation of liberty, threats, economic control and exploitation) by an intimate partner in their lifetime.[56] With regard to sexual assault or sexual violence towards males who are victims of domestic violence, there are "approximately 1 in 71 men in the United States who have reported being raped in his lifetime, which translates to almost 1.6 million men in the United States."[57] There are "8% of men who have experienced sexual violence other than rape (forced to penetrate someone, sexual coercion, unwanted sexual contact, and non-contact unwanted sexual experiences) by an intimate partner at some point in their lifetime."[64]

---

[54] Campbell, Denis (September 5, 2010). *"More than 40% of domestic violence victims are male, report reveals". The Guardian.*
[55] Breiding, M. J., Chen, J. & Black, M. C. (2014). Intimate partner violence in the United States – 2010. Retrieved from http://www.cdc.gov/violenceprevention/pdf/cdc_nisvs_ipv_report_2013_v17_single_a.pdf.
[56] Breiding, M. J., Chen, J. & Black, M. C. (2014). Intimate partner violence in the United States – 2010. Retrieved from http://www.cdc.gov/violenceprevention/pdf/cdc_nisvs_ipv_report_2013_v17_single_a.pdf.
[57] Black, M.C., Basile, K.C., Breiding, M.J., Smith, S.G., Walters, M.L., Merrick, M.T., Chen, J. & Stevens, M. (2011). The national intimate partner and sexual violence survey: 2010 summary report. Retrieved from http://www.cdc.gov/violenceprevention/pdf/nisvs_report2010-a.pdf. [64] National Intimate Partner and Sexual Violence Survey 2010

Remember that domestic violence against men is often experiences by both men and boys in intimate relationships such as dating, living together, married or by a family member. Even though domestic violence is a crime regardless to if the abuser is a male or a female the laws will differ from state to state, jurisdiction to jurisdiction as stated in an earlier chapter. The sad and unfortunate part is that men are not encouraged to report domestic violence against them because of the social stigma that it brings. "Some research has shown that women who assault their male partners are more likely to avoid arrest than men who assault their female partners,[58] due to the fact that female perpetrators of IPV tend to be viewed by law enforcement agencies and the courts as victims.[59] In as such, men may fear that if they do report to the police, they will be assumed to be the abuser, and placed under arrest.[60,61]

The National Crime Council in the Republic of Ireland, reported in a 2005 study that there was an estimated of 5% men who had experienced IPV. These are individuals who had reported that a crime of domestic violence had occurred to the authorities, compared to 29% of women.[69] As far as stalking is concerned, it has been reported that "1 out of every 19 U.S. men have been stalked in their lifetime to the extent that they felt

[58] Felson, Richard B.; Pare, Paul-Philippe (September 2007). *"Does the Criminal Justice System Treat Domestic Violence and Sexual Assault Offenders Leniently?" (PDF)*. Justice Quarterly. *24 (3): 440; 447*.

[59] Kingsnorth, Rodney F.; MacIntosh, Randall C. (September 2007). *"Intimate Partner Violence: The Role of Suspect Gender in Prosecutorial Decision-Making" (PDF)*. Justice Quarterly. *24 (3): 460–494*. *doi:10.1080/07418820701485395*.

[60] Cook, Phillip W. *(1997). Abused Men: The Hidden Side of Domestic Violence*. Westport, CT: Praeger. pp. 43–91. *ISBN 9780313356711*.

[61] Grady, Ann (2002). *"Female-on-Male Domestic Violence: Uncommon or Ignored?"*. In Hoyle, Carolyn; Young, Richard. *New Visions of Crime Victims*. Portland, Oregon: Hart Publishing. pp. 93–95. ISBN 9781841132808. [69] Watson, Dorothy; Parsons, Sara (2005). *Domestic Abuse of Women and Men in Ireland: Report on the National Study of Domestic Abuse (PDF)*. Dublin: National Crime Council of Ireland. p. 169.

very fearful or believed that they or someone close to them would be harmed or killed."[62]

"Among male stalking victims, almost half (44.3%) reported being stalked by only male perpetrators while a similar proportion (46.7%) reported being stalked by only female perpetrators. About 1 in 18 male stalking victims (5.5%) reported having been stalked by both male and female perpetrators in their life."[63]

Hurt, harm and homicide has showed through studies that "between 1980 and 2008, in cases which the victim/offender relationships were known, 7.1% of men were killed by an intimate partner." Similar studies also show that there are "1 in 20 (5%) males that are victims of murder killed by intimate partners."[64] The reason why there are such difficulties in collecting data concerning male victims of domestic violence is that it has been underreported or blatantly omitted from statistical or academic studies. Males underreport because again, the stigma and embarrassment of the role as a male which causes them to become victimize again by society. Even though it is globally recognized that women are more likely than men to be victims of Intimate Partner Violence, the National Crime Victimization Survey reported that "in 2002, 24 percent of U.S. homicides that were as a result of IPV were against men, compared with 76 percent involving women as victims.

---

[62] Black, M.C., Basile, K.C., Breiding, M.J., Smith, S.G., Walters, M.L., Merrick, M.T., Chen, J., & Stevens, M.R. (2011). The national intimate partner and sexual violence survey (NISVS): 2010 summary report. Retrieved from http://www.cdc.gov/violenceprevention/pdf/nisvs_executive_summary-a.pdf.

[63] National Intimate Partner and Sexual Violence Survey 2010

[64] Bridges, F.S., Tatum, K. M., & Kunselman, J.C. (2008). Domestic violence statutes and rates of intimate partner and family homicide: A research note. Criminal Justice Policy Review, 19(1), 117-130. [73] National Intimate Partner and Sexual Violence Survey 2010

Those same studies showed that in 2003, 85 percent of IPV victims were women."[73] Because real men suffer too, in Northern Ireland, the Police Services has campaigned to bring about awareness concerning the severity of male victimization and to promote the reporting of incidents concerning domestic abuse. The country's first shelter for male abuse victims, Men's Aid NI, opened in early 2013. So, it took from 1974 to 2013, 39 years for someone to statistically recognize that male victims of domestic violence actually existed. Chairman Peter Morris has remarked, "Domestic violence against men can take many forms, including emotional, sexual and physical abuse and threats of abuse. It can happen in heterosexual and same-sex relationships and, as with domestic abuse against females, can go largely unreported."[65]. Despite this, there are still very few services that are available to male victims of intimate partner violence.

More men than women were victims of intimate partner physical violence within the past year, according to a national study funded by the Centers for Disease Control and U.S. Department of Justice. According to the National Intimate Partner and Sexual Violence Survey (hereinafter NISVS) they released in December 2011, which noted that within 12 months an estimated 5,365,000 men and 4,741,000 women were victims of intimate partner physical violence. (Black, M.C. et al., 2011, Tables 4.1 and 4.2). This finding contrast to the earlier National Violence Against Women Survey (Tjaden, P. G., & Thoennes, N., 2000) (hereinafter NVAWS), which estimated that 1.2 million women and 835,000 men were victims of intimate partner physical violence in the preceding 12 months. One-year prevalence "are considered to be more accurate [than lifetime rates] because they do not depend on recall of events long past" (Straus, 2005, p. 60).

---

[65] McNeilly, Claire (October 29, 2013). *"Domestic violence against men at its highest level in Northern Ireland since police began recording statistics"*. *Belfast Telegraph.*

Statistics show that in "2013, spousal homicides accounted for 7% of the known murders in California, 60 females were killed, and 4 males were killed."[66] Unfortunately, there are many inconsistencies and limitations in obtaining accurate reporting, because some of numbers that are actually listed may be skewed and may not include unknown murders. "Recent global prevalence figures indicate that 35% of women worldwide have experienced either intimate partner violence or non-partner sexual violence in their lifetime."[67] However, due to inconsistencies and limitations in reporting, the numbers listed may be higher and does not include unknown murders. "From 2003-2012, almost a million Americans (approximately 967,710) were victims of nonfatal violence committed by an intimate partner."[68] "The cost of intimate partner violence in the United States alone exceeds $5.8 billion per year: $4.1 billion is for direct medical and health care services, while productivity losses account for nearly $1.8 billion."[69]

---

[66] (California Department of Justice Division of California Justice Information Services, Bureau of Criminal Information and Analysis Criminal Justice Statistics Center, 2013)
[67] (WHO Media Centre, 2014)
[68] (U.S. Department of Justice – Office of Justice Programs, 2014)
[69] (Department of Health and Human Services Centers for Disease Control and Prevention National Center for Injury Prevention and Control, 2003 & United Nations Secretary-General, 2006)

Chapter 3

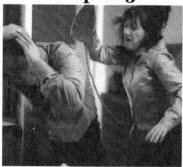

How Domestic Violence Affects Males as Victims

We must be open to our own blinkers and refuse to simplify the complexities of our findings, even if this means we ask questions that might be uncomfortable.[70] Research that is being conducted concerning male victims of domestic violence is not being conducted on a gender-neutral basis. Physically, emotionally, psychologically, and socially domestic violence has an effect on everyone, women, men and their families. For far too long, domestic violence has been framed and understood to be exclusively a women's issue. While most of the attention is given to women who are abused by men, men are often overlooked victims of domestic violence.

According to the Bureau of Justice Statistics Crime Data Brief, men account for approximately 15% of the victims of reported intimate partner violence (February 2003). In a 2010 systematic review of the literature on women's perpetration of IPV, it found that anger, self-defense and retaliation were common motivations but that

---

[70] Stanko, Elizabeth (1997), *"I second that emotion:" Reflections on feminism, emotionality, and research on sexual violence,"* pp. 74-85 in Schwartz, Martin (ed), *Researching Sexual Violence against Women: Methodological and personal perspectives,* Sage, Thousand Oaks, California

distinguishing between self-defense and retaliation was difficult."[71] The truth of the matter is that women who abuse men are not much different than their male counterparts who abuse women.

It appears men can be hit, kicked, punched, pushed, shoved, or bitten by women abusers and that is alright. Women can also use weapons, such as knives, guns, bats, or any object that can they find to be used to strike the man and that too seems to be accepted by many in society. It does not mean that men who are abused are necessarily smaller or physically weaker than the women who abuses them, it just means that some men choose not to hit the woman back for their own reasons. Abused men often do not use their greater size or strength to hurt their abusive partners even when they are being hurt.

Domestic violence affects males in ways that many would not understand, usually because it is hidden and understudied. Being a victim of domestic violence often robs an individual of their ability to maintain the fundamental rights over their own lives. This occurs because those individuals who are abused, they live in constant fear and isolation mostly in the one and only place that they thought they would always feel safe, which is their home. For many victims, regardless to if they are male or female, they must maintain an abundant amount of tremendous courage and strength as they struggle each and every day in order to keep themselves, their children and those who they love safe.

[71] Bair-Merritt, Megan H; Crowne, Sarah Shea; Thompson, Darcy A; Sibinga, Erica; Trent, Maria; Campbell, Jacquelyn (2010). *"Why Do Women Use Intimate Partner Violence? A Systematic Review of Women's Motivations"*. *Trauma, violence & abuse. 11 (4): 178–189.*

Many men are often reluctant to strike a female back because many males know that females can also be manipulative by making it seem as though the male was the initial perpetrator. Some of the manipulative behaviors that females will display are being malicious and spiteful, falsely accusing the male as being a perpetrator, or telling the male that she would get someone to do harm to him or those he loves and letting him know that no one would believe him; she will also add how she could get away with it, even if she has to have him killed. She will withhold sex from him, withhold his children, be deceptive with or about him or even go so far as to seduce him and the try and trap the male by saying that she is expecting so that he would not leave her because she wants him to feel guilty or feel sorry for her. Once he realizes that she was or is lying then the female becomes even more aggressive or abusive. She may then elicit friends or relatives to cause him additional harm which could then lead to hospitalization or even death. All of this is verbal, sexual, emotional, and psychological abuse in order to gain control of the victim.

It should be reiterated that today, research has acknowledged that at least 1 in 7 males have experienced some type of domestic abuse while many will refuse to report the abuse. The effects of domestic violence against men are just as serious as the effects of domestic violence against women, the only difference is that men often suffer in silence. Additional effects can be mental health, depression, and suicide. To think domestic violence is to think about women being beat by their significant other, but today this includes elder abuse, child abuse and female on male abuse as well.

Men usually suffer in silence because they are ashamed and afraid that no one will believe them. Remember how manipulative some females can be? Again, there are those in society who are naive enough to believe that domestic violence against men does not exist, and then there are those who become angry when the subject is brought up, because society is not supposed to care about how the males feel. Their attitude is that "he just needs to suck up his feelings and be a man about it." Understand that no matter what type of abuse is being committed, it is never the victim's fault for the abuser abusing them.

Some tips that males should take concerning domestic violence is that they too are victims and should take being a victim of domestic violence seriously. Because she is a female, the violent behaviors that she may display may seem harmless at first, however, we must remember that the violence can and will escalate. Let her know that the first time she hits you, tell her that there will not be a second time because the second time that she abuses you then you will report the abuse, leave and seek help. Do not take the situation lightly and don't make her think that you are bluffing her, act on it. Do not hit her back, because by you being a man, you can do some serious damage with a single blow. Even trying to physically restrain her is not suggestive, because she can flip the script and say that you were the aggressor, and do not retaliate against her because you will get caught up something that you can't get out of. Remember this, she will eventually get caught or she will display the same behaviors towards someone else who will not take being abused lightly and will have her arrested.

As a male, you shouldn't have to suffer in silence and keep your abusive relationship a secret. Let someone know what is going at home concerning the abuse this way if matters tend to escalate and you are hospitalized, in a coma or you meet your demise then at least you would have told someone like the doctor, a pastor, a counselor, family members, a coworker, friends and have the incident documented and recognized. If you begin speaking about your experiences as a victim of domestic violence, then you can be an advocate to help other males who suffer in silence heal, in addition to allowing society to understand that domestic violence should no longer be perceived as being an issue of women only being abused.

Some of the solutions for assisting males who are victims of domestic violence is to establish shelters and other services for them. The police and judicial system need to realize that males are also victims of domestic violence. Male victims of domestic violence should also be ensured that they too can gain custody of their children or reassured that they will not lose their rights to be a part of their children's lives. Many male victims of domestic violence, like female victims of domestic violence feel that if they leave their significant other than their children will become victimized even more by the violent parent and will be left unprotected. "Evidence suggests that most abused wo/men are not passive victims – they often adopt strategies to maximize their safety and that of their children."[72] Some of the barriers to leaving abuse relationships are, fear, guilt, culture, social norms, love, lack of options, children, lack of support, victim blaming, physical isolation, denial, financial dependence, stalking, harassment, shame and blame, immigration status, religious and spiritual reasons. Some of the family related barriers are, silence about violence, intergenerational violence in family, not offering help when survivor returns to abuser, In-laws taking the side of abuser and battering survivor through children, finances, etc.

Another barrier of domestic violence is shame. What is shame? *"Shame is the intensely painful feeling or experience of believing we are flawed and therefore unworthy of accepting and belonging"* -Brene Brown. Everyone experiences shame,

---

[72] (World Health Organization, Pan Health Organization, 2012)
[82] (Brown, Brené, 2008)

because it is fueled by a culture's expectation of what is acceptable for women and men (gender norms). Shame is about fear which can also lead to blame, powerlessness and disconnection, and can affect mental and physical health."[82]

Then there is a such thing as shame resiliency which "is the ability to recognize shame when it is experienced and move through it in a constructive way that allows individuals to remain authentic, to grow and to overcome shame and its symptoms. Individuals with high levels of shame resilience are able to feel and give more empathy."[73]

Some of the impacts as a result of domestic violence to the victim or survivor can cause several health effects such as chronic pain, gastrointestinal disorders, psychosomatic symptoms, eating problems, unplanned pregnancies, problems during pregnancy, STDs, and/or HIV/AIDS. There can be mental health effects such as, depression, trauma, anxiety, post-traumatic stress disorder, or suicide. And then there are economic health effects such as poverty, and/or homelessness.

Other issues as an occurrence of domestic violence can be reproductive health issues. "IPV may lead to a host of negative sexual and reproductive health consequences for women, including unintended and unwanted pregnancy, abortion and unsafe abortion, sexually transmitted infections including HIV, pregnancy complications, pelvic inflammatory disease, urinary tract infections and sexual dysfunction."[74] "Approximately 6.7% of women in the United States had an intimate partner who

---

[73] (Brown, Brené, 2008)
[74] (Pan American Health Organization - World Health Organization 2012)

refused to use a condom, while 3.8% of men in the United States have had an intimate partner who refused to use a condom."[75]

Other effects could be alcohol and substance abuse. "Although it is difficult to fully determine the link between harmful alcohol and substance abuse, studies show victims of violence may "manage the negative consequences of abuse through the use of alcohol, prescription medication, tobacco or other drugs."[76] Then there are the effects of suicide. "In the WHO multi-country study, there are reports of emotional distress, thoughts of suicide, and attempted suicide were significantly higher among women who had ever experienced physical or sexual violence than those who had not."[77] Homeless as a result of domestic violence. "In 2005, 50 percent of U.S. cities surveyed reported that domestic violence is a primary cause of homelessness."[78] "

A 2003 Florida study found that 46 percent of domestic violence survivors reported that they had experienced homelessness as a result of the violence. Eighty-three percent of survivors reported they had difficulty finding suitable and affordable housing."[79] Some of the impacts that domestic violence can have on family and friends are, risk for their own safety, isolation of victim which leads to their loss of child/friend/relative, and frustration. The impact that domestic violence can have on the community are, dysfunctional families, the victim may be unable to contribute to community, they may experience a loss of employment and healthcare which creates the inability to pay

---

[75] (CDC National Center for Injury Prevention and Control Division of Violence Prevention, 2010)
[76] (WHO United Nations, London School of Hygiene & Tropical Medicine, South African Medical Research Council, 2013)
[77] (Pan American Health Organization - World Health Organization 2012)
[78] (American Civil Liberties Union, 2008)
[79] American Civil Liberties Union, 2008

the costs of being in a safe environment which forces them to move in an area where there is a high rate of crime.

Societal attitudes are that men are more violent than women, but some of the main reasons for women becoming violent is because she is jealous that the male is giving his time more to the children, or to his family and friends and which is one of the reasons for the isolation. Some females want to control the male's behavior by threatening bodily harm even death, "if I can't have you, no one will." She will place the blame on other people or circumstances for the problems that the two of you are having, she will say cruel, evil, and hurtful things to you or even your children, she will have sudden mood swings or unpredictable behaviors. She will throw things or breaks things, or even destroy things that belongs to you. She will even use force to begin arguments, she may try to hold you down, push, slap, or shove you. These types of behaviors are not behaviors that are displayed only by males, these are the warning signs of all batterers.

We know that women suffer grievously when a man beats them, children suffer as well, but we must never underestimate the horrible effects of domestic violence towards anyone, including males, because there are two sides to the story as men who are victims suffer the same fate. Society can't just examine the bits and pieces of domestic violence as being a female only victim, society must examine all of the aspects of domestic violence. The truth is that women, just like men, can initiate violence just as often as men. Batterers come in both sexes, so society's attitudes should not be gender biased but be gender neutral. Public perceptions should be that there are those men who can be passive victims and that there can be women who are violent creatures.

The way in which many are affected concerning domestic violence is because of the limited services that is provided for them such as those who are not served or are underserved. This includes, African Americans, those of Latin or Latina decent, Asian and Pacific Islander, Middle Eastern, People with disabilities, LGBTQ population, people with substance abuse issues, and people with mental health issues. The information that has been obtained concerning IPV in the areas of those who are the unserved or underserved populations are limited due to the inconsistencies and unreliability of data. These less served populations often experience stereotypes and discrimination which impacts how or if they receive services. Society's cultural values, their norms, and societies traditions will often impact how less served populations will experience IPV.

It should be briefly noted that according to the research that has been collected and the individuals experience, trans individuals experience IPV at a greater rate of 25%-33% than non-trans individuals.[80] "Lesbian women and gay men reported levels of intimate partner violence and sexual violence equal to or higher than those of heterosexuals."[81] "American Indians experience violent victimization at a rate greater than other U.S. racial or ethnic subgroups."[82] Those who are the most vulnerable to IVP are teens, those who are pregnant, those who are in physical isolation, those who are non-English speakers, those with mental health issues, those with disabilities, LGBTQ and male victims of domestic abuse.

Male victims just as female victims also experience trauma as a result of domestic violence. "Traumatic events produced profound and lasting changes in physiological arousal, emotion, cognition, and memory. Trauma is defined as: helplessness, intense

---

[80] (Munson, Michael, Forge, National Resource Center on Domestic Violence, 2014)
[81] The National Intimate Partner and Sexual Violence Survey (NISVS), 2010)
[82] (Wahab, Stéphanie, Ph.D., and Lenora Olson, M.A., 2014)

fear, loss of control, threat of annihilation or death."[83] "Trauma affects, the amygdala which is the "doing" part of the brain. This alerts the brain when there is danger. Cerebrum – is the "thinking" part of the brain. This helps the brain problem solve, think things though, etc. In response to danger, the cerebrum shuts down, and the amygdala takes over resulting in flight, fight or freeze. This response effects memory, smell, touch, etc. Our brain bodies are designed to remember the dangers we experience as a survival mechanism.

Triggers results in when an event happens that reminds the brain of a past danger and the body reacts in response."[84] "Domestic violence differs from other traumatic experiences. [Because] domestic violence is, by its nature, chronic [and] the perpetrator of the traumatic experience is a loved one."[85] "As a result, victims experiencing domestic violence may exhibit a range of 'flight, fight or freeze' behaviors. *Examples: hyperarousal, intrusion or re-experiencing events, and constriction or avoidance.*"[96] There are studies which shows that in the past, instances such as these are also considered to result in Trauma Bonding or Stockholm Syndrome. Researchers must stop telling half-truths.

[83] (Judith Lewis Herman "Trauma and Recovery", 1997)
[84] (Ohio Domestic Violence Network, Judith Lewis Herman "Trauma and Recovery", 1997)
[85] (Ohio Domestic Violence Network, Judith Lewis Herman "Trauma and Recovery", 1997)
[96] (Ohio Domestic Violence Network, Judith Lewis Herman "Trauma and Recovery", 1997)

Chapter 4

Domestic Violence, Our Youth, and Children, and Nipping It the Bud

With early intervention and education, advocates can prevent and nip in the bud the negative and adverse effects of domestic violence. Society must understand that those youth who are exposed to domestic violence are at a greater risk for being both a victim and the perpetrator of future dating violence. Classroom-level interventions were delivered in six sessions, using a curriculum emphasizing the consequences for perpetrators, state laws and penalties, the construction of gender roles, and healthy relationships.

Educational intervention means that school-level interventions included the use of temporary school-based restraining orders, higher levels of faculty and security presence in "hot spots," and raising awareness about domestic violence schoolwide. Researchers found that, compared with the control group who received no intervention, students who received the school-level intervention or both the school and classroom level of interventions many schools experienced reduced levels of dating violence and sexual harassment. The researchers noted that the classroom-level intervention alone was not effective in improving these outcomes. In addition, students in the school-level intervention were more likely to intend to intervene as bystanders if they witnessed abusive behavior between their peers.[86] The reason why such findings are important in many ways:

•   This is one of the first studies to document the effectiveness of such prevention programs among middle school students.

•   Given the large size of the study (with more than 2,500 students) and the ethnic diversity of these students, the program may be applicable to a broad range of populations.

•   The success of the school-level intervention is particularly important because it can be implemented with very few extra costs to schools.[87]

Then there are family-based interventions for high risks youth where the intervention will be able to assist families to recognize the effects of domestic violence and understand that domestic violence is an issue. Such interventions will allow youth who are exposed to domestic violence to realize that they are at increased risk to be both a victim and perpetrator of dating violence. Yet there are currently no violence intervention protocols for this vulnerable group. In order to help fill these gaps, the NIJ has funded an effort to adapt the successes of an existing evidence-based program, Families for Safe Dates, so that it would be applicable to teens who are exposed to domestic violence.

---

[86] Taylor, Bruce, Nan D. Stein, Dan Woods, and Elizabeth Mumford. *Shifting Boundaries: Final Report on an Experimental Evaluation of a Youth Dating Violence Prevention Program in New York City Middle Schools (pdf, 322 pages)*. Final report submitted to the National Institute of Justice, grant number 2008-MU-MU-0010, October 2011, NCJ 236175.

[87] See the curriculum evaluated in this study, *Shifting Boundaries: Lessons on Relationships for Students in Middle School (pdf, 65 pages)*.

In order to adapt Families for Safe Dates for teens who are exposed to domestic violence, the researcher recruited 28 women (and 35 of their 12- to 15-year-old children) from four counties, either when the women were in court filing a domestic violence protection order or when the women were seeking services through public or community-based programs. In order for the participant to be eligible for the program, women had to have been victims of domestic violence but no longer living with their partners and they had to have a child 12 to 15-year-old.[88]

There are many factors that will influence a child's responses to domestic violence, because not all children are affected the way. There are some children who do not show obvious signs of stress, or they have learned how to develop their own coping mechanisms. Then there are those children who may be more affected than other children.[89] The ways in which some children are effected by domestic violence depends upon the "child's age, their experiences, if they have had a prior trauma history, and their temperament all which have an influence on how a child is affected.[90] "For example, an adolescent who grows up in an atmosphere of repeated acts of violence may have different posttraumatic stress reactions than a 12-year-old who has witnessed a single violent fight. A six-year-old girl who saw her mother bleeding on the floor and

---

[88] Ehrensaft, Miriam K., Patricia Cohen, Jocelyn Brown, Elizabeth Smailes, Henian Chen, and Jeffrey G. Johnson. "Intergenerational Transmission of Partner Violence: A 20-Year Prospective Study," *Journal of Counseling and Clinical Psychology* 71 (August 2003): 741-753.

[89] Domestic Violence and Children: Questions and Answers for Domestic Violence Project Advocates November 2010. Copyright © 2010, National Center for Child Traumatic Stress on behalf of Rebecca Brown, LCSW, Faye Luppi, JD, and the National Child Traumatic Stress Network. The National Child Traumatic Stress Network 11 www.NCTSN.org

[90] Domestic Violence and Children: Questions and Answers for Domestic Violence Project Advocates November 2010. Copyright © 2010, National Center for Child Traumatic Stress on behalf of Rebecca Brown, LCSW, Faye Luppi, JD, and the National Child Traumatic Stress Network. The National Child Traumatic Stress Network 11 www.NCTSN.org

feared she would die would likely have more of a severe reaction than a child who has perceived the incident she witnessed to be less dangerous."[91] "A child's proximity to the violence also makes a difference. Consider the very different experiences of a 12-year-old child who was in another room with headphones on while her parents battled; then look at an eight-year-old who had to call 911 despite a raging parent's threats against him; then you have a teenager who has frequently put himself at risk by getting into the middle of fights to protect his mother from her estranged boyfriend,"[92] or a father from an estranged girlfriend.

When you have adults in the family that are under stress then you will have children that are under stress whether you may believe this to be true. If you have never thought about it, then think about it now. Child abuse and domestic violence often occur in the same family. "Researchers have found that 50 percent to 70 percent of the men who frequently assaulted their wives also frequently abused their children,"[93] the same holds true for wives who assault their husbands, they too often abuse their children. "The UN Secretary-General's Study on Violence Against Children conservatively estimates that 275 million children worldwide are exposed to violence in the home."[94] Witnessing violence between one's parents or caretakers is the strongest risk factor of transmitting the violent behavior from one generation to the next.[95]

---

[91] Domestic Violence and Children: Questions and Answers for Domestic Violence Project Advocates
[92] Domestic Violence and Children: Questions and Answers for Domestic Violence Project Advocates
November 2010. Copyright © 2010, National Center for Child Traumatic Stress on behalf of Rebecca Brown, LCSW, Faye Luppi, JD, and the National Child Traumatic Stress Network. The National Child Traumatic Stress Network 11 www.NCTSN.org
[93] (Futures Without Violence, The facts on Children and Domestic Violence, 2008)
[94] (Futures Without Violence, The facts on Children and Domestic Violence, 2008)
[95] (National Coalition Against Domestic Violence, Domestic Violence Facts, 2007) November 2010. Copyright © 2010, National Center for Child Traumatic Stress on behalf of Rebecca Brown,

There are some children who witness domestic violence in the household that can have some influencing factors that will help them to overcome a learned behavior of domestic violence, thereby breaking the cycle. Some of those factors can be, gender, age, support from a significant adult, the frequency and severity of the abuse, the proximity and disposition of the child.[96] However, some of the challenges that a child may face may be, social, emotional, psychological, behavioral as well as physical. Some of the things that children can see, hear or feel by age can be prenatally, infants and toddlers, childhood and teen years. Some of the prenatal challenges can be, direct fetal injury, late prenatal care, pre-term labor, placental abruption, exposure to substance abuse alcohol/tobacco, low birth weight, and vomiting.[97]

Some of the challenges that infants and toddlers face are, problems with eating, the failure to thrive, having problems bedwetting and constant nightmares, being incorrigible, having withdrawals or being passive, excessively seeking attention, being manipulative, having a greater need for dependency and having constant mood swings.[98] Some of the emotional and psychological challenges that infants and toddlers also face are, having difficulty sleeping, at such a young age having shame, guilt and self-blame, experiencing confusion about conflicting feelings towards their parents, having a fear of abandonment, and having anger issues.[99] Some of the social challenges that infants and toddlers face are, attachment problems, lack of responsiveness, poor anger

LCSW, Faye Luppi, JD, and the National Child Traumatic Stress Network. The National Child Traumatic Stress Network 11 www.NCTSN.org

[96] California Partnership to End Domestic Violence (2012). Cpedv.org.
[97] California Partnership to End Domestic Violence (2012). Cpedv.org.
[98] California Partnership to End Domestic Violence (2012). Cpedv.org.
[99] California Partnership to End Domestic Violence (2012). Cpedv.org.

management and problem solving skills.[100] Some of the physical challenges that infants and toddlers face are, developmental disabilities, language delays, injuries when caught in the crossfire, having a short attention span, always being tired and lethargic, constantly being ill, having poor personal hygiene, and self-abuse.[101]

Some of the childhood challenges which can be emotional and psychological can be, depression, shame, guilt, and self-blame, they too can experience confusion about conflicting feelings towards parents, have serious anger issues, experience feelings of helplessness and powerlessness and embarrassment.[102] Some of the social challenges that children face are, having inadequate social skill development, having extreme separation anxiety, being isolated from friends and relatives, having difficulty in trusting, especially adults, having poor anger management and problem solving skills and passivity with peers, or bullying.[103] Some of the physical challenges that some of these children face are, being frequently ill, having somatic complaints, headaches and stomachaches, they are always nervous, anxious, and have a short attention span, they are always tired and lethargic, they have poor personal hygiene habits, they have a regression in development, there is a high risk play and they demonstrate signs of self-abuse.

Further studies indicate that children and youth are 1,500 times more likely to be abused in homes where partner abuse occurs. As mentioned earlier, domestic violence may result in physical injury, psychological and emotional harm, verbal abuse, sexual abuse or the neglect of children. There is most definitely a correlation between family

---

[100] California Partnership to End Domestic Violence (2012). Cpedv.org.
[101] California Partnership to End Domestic Violence (2012). Cpedv.org.
[102] California Partnership to End Domestic Violence (2012). Cpedv.org.
[103] California Partnership to End Domestic Violence (2012). Cpedv.org.

domestic violence and juvenile delinquency. It is also likely that children have a six times greater chance of committing suicide, with a 24 percent greater chance of committing sexual assault crimes while another 50 percent have a greater likelihood of abusing drugs and alcohol.[104]

One of the most tragic outcomes of domestic violence is that well more than half of the young men between the ages of 11 and 22 who are in jail for homicide have killed their mother's batterer. Children growing up in violent homes do not need to be physically abused to take on violent and delinquent behavior — it is enough to witness their mother's abuse.[105] It must also be recognized that in many cases, globally, children who witness their fathers being abused have demonstrated some of the same types of behaviors. "What men learn as boys, they do as men. That is why we need to teach our sons and other boys in our lives that violence against women is wrong. Now, when they need to hear it most."[117] That's the message behind "Teach Early", the new public education campaign sponsored by the Family Violence Prevention Fund (FVPF) and The Advertising Council.

With this new campaign it encourages fathers, coaches, teachers, uncles and mentors to shape the attitudes and behaviors of boys.[106] "Violent behavior is learned, and men have the power to teach boys that violence against women is wrong," said FVPF President Esta Soler.[107] Even where boys, rather than men, are considered, there

[104] (National Coalition Against Domestic Violence, Domestic Violence Facts, 2007)
[105] (National Coalition Against Domestic Violence, Domestic Violence Facts, 2007)
[117] Family Violence Prevention Fund (FVPF) and The Advertising Council.
[106] Family Violence Prevention Fund (FVPF) and The Advertising Council.
[107] Source: endabuse.org/newsflash/index.php3?Search=Article&NewsFlashID=316

is a comparable trend. When boys are sexually abused, the perpetrator is less likely to be a family member than is the case when girls are sexually abused.[108],[109]

Some of the short-term responses that some children faces are "Hyperarousal. This is where the child may become jumpy, nervous, or easily startled. The child may also experience some issues of reexperiencing the negative behaviors. The child may continue to see or relive images, sensations, or memories of the domestic violence despite trying to put them out of their mind. The child may avoid situations, people, and reminders that are associated with the violence, or may try not to think or talk about it.

The child may feel numb, frozen, or shut down, they may feel and act as if cut off from normal life and other people. The child may react to any reminder of the domestic violence. These reminders can be things that are associated with sights, smells, tastes, sounds, words, things, places, emotions, or even other people who can become linked in the child's mind with the traumatic events. For example, a school-age child may become upset when watching a football game because the violent contact between players is a reminder of domestic violence.[110]

Sometimes the behaviors that some children seem to display may come out of nowhere, such as a sudden tantrum, which is actually a reaction to a trauma reminder. The child may have trouble going to sleep or staying asleep or they may be having

---

[108] See, for example, Bolton et al (1989: 45). However, as with research on other forms of sexual assault, data on the sexual abuse of boys generally dispels the myth that boys are most at risk from strangers. The key difference between boys and girls here appears to be that, comparatively, boys are more likely to beat risk from males they know in some way but to whom they are not related.

[109] Bolton, Frank, Morris, Larry and MacEachron, Ann (1989). "*Males at Risk: The other side of child sexual abuse.*" Sage, Newbury Park, California

[110] Domestic Violence and Children: Questions and Answers for Domestic Violence Project Advocates November 2010. Copyright © 2010, National Center for Child Traumatic Stress on behalf of Rebecca Brown, LCSW, Faye Luppi, JD, and the National Child Traumatic Stress Network. The National Child Traumatic Stress Network 11 www.NCTSN.org

nightmares. The child may also display repetitive talk or play about the domestic violence. For example, a young girl may act out violence when playing with her dolls. Other short-term symptoms may include anxiety (for example, separation anxiety); depression; aggression (perhaps reenactment of the witnessed aggression); physical complaints (stomachaches, headaches); behavioral problems (fighting, oppositional behavior, tantrums); feelings of guilt or self-blame; and poor academic performance.[111]

Some responses from children according to "research suggests that in the long term, children who have been exposed to domestic violence—especially those children who do not receive therapeutic intervention,"[112] they may be subjected to an increased risk of depression and anxiety, they may become substance abuser, or display self-destructive or suicidal behaviors; these children may also demonstrate impulsive acts, including risky sex and unintended pregnancy, they may experience chronic health problems or develop low self-esteem, they may also demonstrate criminalistics and violent behaviors (including perpetration of domestic violence), or they themselves may also experience victimization by an intimate partner later in life.[113]

There are some of the factors that will help children to recover from the trauma of domestic violence. Because many "children are resilient if given the proper help

---

[111] Domestic Violence and Children: Questions and Answers for Domestic Violence Project Advocates November 2010. Copyright © 2010, National Center for Child Traumatic Stress on behalf of Rebecca Brown, LCSW, Faye Luppi, JD, and the National Child Traumatic Stress Network. The National Child Traumatic Stress Network 11 www.NCTSN.org

[112] Domestic Violence and Children: Questions and Answers for Domestic Violence Project Advocates November 2010. Copyright © 2010, National Center for Child Traumatic Stress on behalf of Rebecca Brown, LCSW, Faye Luppi, JD, and the National Child Traumatic Stress Network. The National Child Traumatic Stress Network 11 www.NCTSN.org

[113] Domestic Violence and Children: Questions and Answers for Domestic Violence Project Advocates November 2010. Copyright © 2010, National Center for Child Traumatic Stress on behalf of Rebecca Brown, LCSW, Faye Luppi, JD, and the National Child Traumatic Stress Network. The National Child Traumatic Stress Network 11 www.NCTSN.org

following their traumatic experiences, they will have the ability to recover and break the cycle of domestic violence. Research has shown that the support of family and community are key to increasing children's capacity for resilience and in helping them to recover and thrive."[114] Some of the things that are extremely crucial to a child's resiliency is the child knowing that they have the "presence of a positive, caring, and protective adult in a child's life. Although a long-term relationship with a caregiver is best, even a brief relationship with one caring adult—a mentor, teacher, day-care provider, an advocate in a domestic violence shelter—can make an important difference.[115]

Some important and protective factors for children include, "access to positive social supports (religious organizations, clubs, sports, group activities, teachers, coaches, mentors, day care providers, and others). Children of such traumatic experiences should also be around individuals who are average to above average and intellectually developed with good attention and social skills, a mentor should pay attention to the child's competence at doing something that attracts the praise and admiration of other adults and peers. If that child has an interest in something that they enjoy doing then encourage their goals, dreams and aspirations. Allow them to express

---

[114] Edleson, J. L., in consultation with Nissley, B. (2006). *Emerging responses to children exposed to domestic violence*. Harrisburg, PA: VANet, of the National Resource Center on Domestic Violence/Pennsylvania Coalition Against Domestic Violence. Retrieved April 22, 2018, from: http://www.vawnet.org

[115] Domestic Violence and Children: Questions and Answers for Domestic Violence Project Advocates November 2010. Copyright © 2010, National Center for Child Traumatic Stress on behalf of Rebecca Brown, LCSW, Faye Luppi, JD, and the National Child Traumatic Stress Network. The National Child Traumatic Stress Network 11 www.NCTSN.org

positive feelings of self-esteem and self-efficacy, and encourage their religious affiliations, or spiritual beliefs that gives meaning to life.[116]

There are some parents who may be reluctant to tell someone that their children have witnessed domestic violence, while others may try to minimize their children's actual exposure to the violence (saying, for example, "They didn't know it was happening," or "They were always asleep or at school."[117] A parent who has been victimized will do all that they can to try avoiding speaking to their child about domestic violence. Oftentimes that parent may assume that a child is too young to understand, or that it's better to just move on.[118] Unfortunately there are many children who have experienced domestic violence who may actually want to talk about it, because they are reaching out. "There are some children who may misunderstand what happened or why it happened. They may blame themselves, blame the victim, or blame the police or other authorities who intervened. They may have fantasies about how they can "fix" their family. They may take parental silence as a signal to keep silent themselves or to feel ashamed about what happened in their family."[119]

---

[116] Domestic Violence and Children: Questions and Answers for Domestic Violence Project Advocates November 2010. Copyright © 2010, National Center for Child Traumatic Stress on behalf of Rebecca Brown, LCSW, Faye Luppi, JD, and the National Child Traumatic Stress Network. The National Child Traumatic Stress Network 11 www.NCTSN.org

[117] Domestic Violence and Children: Questions and Answers for Domestic Violence Project Advocates November 2010. Copyright © 2010, National Center for Child Traumatic Stress on behalf of Rebecca Brown, LCSW, Faye Luppi, JD, and the National Child Traumatic Stress Network. The National Child Traumatic Stress Network 11 www.NCTSN.org

[118] Domestic Violence and Children: Questions and Answers for Domestic Violence Project Advocates November 2010. Copyright © 2010, National Center for Child Traumatic Stress on behalf of Rebecca Brown, LCSW, Faye Luppi, JD, and the National Child Traumatic Stress Network. The National Child Traumatic Stress Network 11 www.NCTSN.org

[119] Domestic Violence and Children: Questions and Answers for Domestic Violence Project Advocates November 2010. Copyright © 2010, National Center for Child Traumatic Stress on behalf of Rebecca Brown, LCSW, Faye Luppi, JD, and the National Child Traumatic Stress Network. The National Child Traumatic Stress Network 11 www.NCTSN.org

When responding to children who have witnessed domestic violence, the responsible adult must provide that child with love and care, trust and respect, emotional security, physical security, discipline, time, attention, affection, encouragement and support, and taking care of yourself.[120] As you connect with children who have witnessed domestic violence, frequently remind the child that the violence is not their fault, and there is nothing they could have done to prevent it, avoid making negative statements about the batterer, but provide support, encouragement, and patience. As the advocator, pay attention to nonverbal communication, model appropriate behavior, and allow them to talk about their feelings and don't label them, help them to identify coping skills. Use language which focuses on the child, not your opinion of the child. Instead of saying "I'm proud of you" say "You're doing great." These are just some of the ways that you can help the family is by using the empowerment model and by using family centered approaches. [121]

Some of the safety planning tips that you can use for children of abuse and their families are, pretend that they are in an unsafe home, and have only five minutes to gather their belongings before leaving. Consider the 20 items listed on your worksheet and rank them based on level of importance (1 = the most important item to take with you, and 20 = the least important item). Continue positive reinforcement that will allow the family of domestic violence to begin the healing process.

---

[120] California Partnership to End Domestic Violence (2012). Cpedv.org.
[121] California Partnership to End Domestic Violence (2012). Cpedv.org.

Chapter 5

Teen Domestic Violence (TDV), How are They Affected

The ultimate goal of prevention and intervention is to stop teen domestic violence and dating violence before it begins. During the preteen and teen years, young people are learning the skills that they need in order to form positive, and healthy relationships with others. This is an ideal time during their lives to promote healthy relationships and prevent patterns of relationship violence that can last well into adulthood.[122] Studies investigating the effectiveness of programs to prevent dating violence are beginning to show positive results. Most programs focus on changing knowledge by bringing about awareness concerning domestic violence, they focus on the attitudes and behaviors that are linked with dating violence while focusing on the skills that are needed to build healthy relationships.[123] In one rigorous NIJ-funded study, school-level interventions in 30 New York City public middle schools stated that the intervention programs reduced dating violence by up to 50 percent.[136] Researchers evaluated dating violence and sexual harassment interventions by randomly assigning classes to receive: Classroom-level

---

[122] Centers for Disease Control and Prevention. *"Understanding Teen Dating Violence."*
[123] Centers for Disease Control and Prevention. *"Understanding Teen Dating Violence."*
[136] Centers for Disease Control and Prevention. *"Understanding Teen Dating Violence."*

interventions, School-level interventions, A combination of classroom- and school-level interventions, No intervention (i.e., the control group).[124]

These studies showed that adolescents who are maltreated and become involved in the child welfare system are more at risk for being revictimized by romantic partners.[125] To better understand how to prevent revictimization among this high-risk group, NIJ funded a study to evaluate the effectiveness of two prevention curriculums. The study focused on girls because they sometimes girls faced more serious consequences of dating violence (e.g., injuries, pregnancy) than boys did.[126] Among adult victims of rape, physical violence, and/ or stalking by an intimate partner, 22% of women and 15% of men first experienced some form of partner violence between 11 and 17 years of age.[127]

What is teen domestic violence and how are teens affected? Teen dating abuse, which may also be referred to as teen dating violence, means the physical, sexual, verbal, emotional, or technological conduct that is directed towards a person by a person in order to harm, threaten, intimidate, or control a dating partner, regardless of whether

[124] Taylor, Bruce, Nan D. Stein, Dan Woods, and Elizabeth Mumford. *Shifting Boundaries: Final Report on an Experimental Evaluation of a Youth Dating Violence Prevention Program in New York City Middle Schools (pdf, 322 pages).* Final report submitted to the National Institute of Justice, grant number 2008-MU-MU-0010, October 2011, NCJ 236175.
[125] Coker, Ann L., Robert E. McKeown, Maureen Sanderson, Keith E. Davis, Robert F. Valois, and E. Scott Huebner, "Severe Dating Violence and Quality of Life Among South Carolina High School Students," *American Journal of Preventative Medicine* 19 (November 2000): 220-227.
[126] Silverman, Jay G., Anita Raj, Lorelei A. Mucci, and Jeanne E. Hathaway, "Dating Violence Against Adolescent Girls and Associated Substance Use, Unhealthy Weight Control, Sexual Risk Behavior, Pregnancy, and Suicidality," *Journal of the American Medical Association* 286 (August 2001): 572-579.
[127] Vagi, K. J., Olsen, E. O., Basile, K. C., & Vivolo-Kantor, A. M. (2015). Teen dating violence (physical and sexual) among US high school students: Findings from the 2013 National Youth Risk Behavior Survey. JAMA Pediatrics, 169, 474-482.

that relationship is continuing or has concluded. It does not matter the number of interactions that were between the individuals that were involved, such instances still can happen. Such abuses may include insults, coercion, social sabotage, sexual harassment, threats and/or acts of physical or sexual violence.[128] A 2017 CDC Report found that approximately 7% of women and 4% of men who ever experienced rape, physical violence, or stalking by an intimate partner first experienced some form of partner violence by that partner before 18 years of age. The 2013 National Youth Risk Behavior Survey found approximately 10% of high school students reported physical victimization and 10% reported sexual victimization from a dating partner in the 12 months before they were surveyed.

Some of the things that many teens hear who are in an abusive relationship is, "You should be grateful I even put up with you," "You know that I can't live without you," "You belong to me.... if I can't have you," "If you leave, I don't know what I might do......." "If you leave me, I'm going to kill myself!" "Why didn't you answer your phone? You must have been out with someone else!"[129] Such statements are learned behaviors of domestic violence from an emotional, psychological, and verbal perspective. "More than 1 in 3 teens have reported that their partners wanted to know where they were and who they were with all the times."[130] "Nearly 1 in 3 teens who have been in relationships have experienced the most serious forms of dating abuse and violence including sexual violence physical violence, or threats of physical harm to a partner or to themselves."[131]

---

[128] California Partnership to End Domestic Violence (2012). Cpedv.org.
[129] California Partnership to End Domestic Violence (2012). Cpedv.org.
[130] Liz Claiborne Inc. and National Teen Dating Abuse Helpline study on teen & teen dating abuse conducted by Teenage Research Unlimited, February 2008.
[131] Liz Claiborne Inc. and Family Abuse Prevention Fund study on teen dating abuse & abuse linked to the troubled economy conducted by Teenage Research Unlimited, June 2009

Some of the attitudes and exceptions that teen offenders may believe is that, they have the right to "control" their partners by any means necessary. Some male offenders may also believe that aggressiveness, according to cultural and traditional perspectives are "masculine" and submission is "feminine." However, this can go both ways where the feminist is the aggressor and feels that the male should be the submissive one. The teen aggressor also feels as though they "possess" their partner or that they have the right to demand intimacy. These abusers may also feel that they may lose respect from their peers if they are too attentive and supportive of their partner.[132]

Teen survivors may believe that they are responsible for solving the problems they are having in their relationships, and that their partner is not responsible for the problems that they are having. Survivor's may also feel that their partners jealousy, possessiveness, and even physical abuse, is part of the "romantic" behavior which is part of the relationship. The victim of such abusive treatments also feel that they should tolerate or accept the violent behavior if their partner pays for things or buy the victims love. Survivors may also feel that their partner's jealous behavior means he/she loves them and that such abuse is "normal" because their friends are also being abused. The last resort for the victim may be that the victim may feel that there is no one for them to go to and ask for help.[133]

[132] Domestic Violence and Children: Questions and Answers for Domestic Violence Project Advocates November 2010. Copyright © 2010, National Center for Child Traumatic Stress on behalf of Rebecca Brown, LCSW, Faye Luppi, JD, and the National Child Traumatic Stress Network. The National Child Traumatic Stress Network 11 www.NCTSN.org
[133] Domestic Violence and Children: Questions and Answers for Domestic Violence Project Advocates November 2010. Copyright © 2010, National Center for Child Traumatic Stress on behalf of Rebecca Brown, LCSW, Faye Luppi, JD, and the National Child Traumatic Stress Network. The National Child Traumatic Stress Network 11 www.NCTSN.org

Societal attitudes concerning teen dating violence is that many do not realize that abusive and unhealthy behaviors are extremely common in teenage relationships. "In fact, one in three adolescent girls in the United States have revealed that they are a victim of *physical, emotional* or *verbal abuse* from a dating partner."[134]

Teens must understand that dating abuse is never their fault when they are the victim. They must also understand that as a survivor it is not them who provokes "dating abuse by making their partner jealous, act mean, or tease their partner into believing they want to have sex. Perpetrators of dating abuse are always responsible for their actions, regardless of the victim's behavior."[148] The truth is that jealous and possessive behaviors are signs that your partner sees you as a possession, not that they love you. These are the most common and early warning signs of abuse."[135]

Just for informational purposes "teens in same-sex relationships experience rates of abuse and violence similar to rates experienced by teens in heterosexual relationships. Nearly one in four teens and young adults (ages 12-21 years) in same-sex romantic or sexual relationships reported some type of partner abuse victimization in the past year-and-a half. One in ten reported experiencing physical abuse by a dating partner."[136] "Dating abuse is very common among young teens, or "tweens. One in five tweens – ages 11 to 14 – say that many of their friends are survivors of dating abuse and nearly half who are in relationships know friends who are verbally abused. Two in five of

---

[134] (Davis, Antoinette, MPH. 2008. Interpersonal and Physical Dating abuse among Teens. The National Council on Crime and Delinquency Focus. Available at
http://www.nccdcrc.org/nccd/pubs/Dating%20abuse%20Among%20Teens.pdf.)
[148] California Partnership to End Domestic Violence (2012). Cpedv.org.
[135] California Partnership to End Domestic Violence (2012). Cpedv.org.
[136] (Halpern CT, Young ML, Waller MW, Martin SL & Kupper LL. 2004. Prevalence of Partner abuse in Same-sex. Romantic and Sexual Relationships in a National Sample of Adolescents. *Journal of Adolescent Health. 35(2): 124-131.*)

the youngest tweens, ages 11 and 12, report that their friends are survivors of verbal abuse in relationships."[137]

Society has this attitude that middle school youth are too young to learn about dating abuse because they aren't dating yet."[152] However, the truth of the matter is that dating abuse does not happen because offenders can't control their tempers. Offenders are able to control their tempers around teachers, supervisors, and authority figures. They choose to be abusive with their dating partners."[138] "Teen dating abuse can be very dangerous and sometimes lethal." Nationwide, nearly one in ten high-school students (9.8 percent) has been *hit, slapped or physically hurt* on purpose by a boyfriend or girlfriend."[139]

The common societal attitudes about teen domestic violence is that teen dating abuse isn't dangerous. People think that it is mostly just arguing and kids goofing around. However, the truth of the matter is that the abuse happens in many ways other than physical abuse. Abuse can be verbal, spiritual, and even financial. Put-downs, insults, and controlling behavior are just as abusive as hitting. Societal attitudes also suggest that if the offender isn't hitting their partner, then it isn't really abuse. Some of the warning signs and effects of teen dating abuse are that the abuser was or is being abused by a parent. The abuser grew up in a home with domestic violence.

[137] (Tween and Teen Dating abuse and abuse Study, Teenage Research Unlimited for Liz Claiborne Inc. and the National Teen Dating Abuse Helpline. February 2008. Available athttp://www.loveisnotabuse.com/pdf/Tween%20Dating%20abuse%20Full%20Report.pdf.)
[152] California Partnership to End Domestic Violence (2012). Cpedv.org.
[138] California Partnership to End Domestic Violence (2012). Cpedv.org.
[139] (Eaton DK, Kann L, Kinchen S, et al. 2010. Youth Risk Behavior Surveillance --- United States, 2009. *Morbidity and Mortality Weekly Report.* 59(SS5);1-148. Available at http://www.cdc.gov/mmwr/pdf/ss/ss5905.pdf.)

The abuser gets very serious in relationships very quickly. The abuser is extremely charming, and an overly smooth talker or they are extremely jealous. The abuser isolates their partner from support systems and attempts to control their partner's behaviors. The abuser is abusive or violent towards other people or animals and blames others for their misbehaviors or failures. The abuser may or does abuse drugs or alcohol or has unrealistic expectations, such as wanting partner to meet all of their needs and be perfect.[140] Some of the effects of dating abuse is associated with the abuser or victim having a significantly higher rate of eating disorder behaviors, they usually have lower self-esteem issues, or higher rates of suicide attempts or lower levels of emotional wellbeing.[141] Once a teenager has realized that they are in an abusive relationship, what they must do to elevate their relationship is to choose a relationship that they can evaluate. This may be a current or former dating relationship, or relationship with a friend or family member.[142]

Some of the dynamics of teen dating abuse are that teens may use physical, sexual, verbal, emotional, or technological conduct to harm, threaten, intimidate, or control a dating partner. Some of the common tactics that teen abusers use is isolating the victim from their friends and trying to isolate them from their family. These abusers will often display bouts of extreme jealousy while also using intimidation tactics such as putting the victim down in front of others, they will use tactics of fear, threats and stalking.[143]

---

[140] California Partnership to End Domestic Violence (2012). Cpedv.org.
[141] (American Bar Association, 2004)
[142] California Partnership to End Domestic Violence (2012). Cpedv.org.
[143] California Partnership to End Domestic Violence (2012). Cpedv.org.

Many teens have a fear of reporting. Teens in abusive relationships are often afraid to report the abuse for various reasons such as because they are in fear of retaliation, they fear that adults won't believe them, or they are afraid that the incident will be reported to Child Family Services and they will be removed from their home, or they are afraid of being outed or ridiculed by their peers or even family.[144] When it comes to teen domestic violence and how they are affected, we must first focus on teen dating. Dating violence is widespread as it has some serious long-term as well as short-term effects. Many teens do not report the abuse because they are afraid to tell friends and family. Studies concerning teen dating violence shows that "13.4% of male high school students report being physically or sexually abused by a dating partner."[145]

There was a study done in 2006 conducted by The International Dating Violence Study, which investigated IPV amongst 13,601 students across thirty-two-nations and found that "about one-quarter of both male and female students had been physically attacked by a partner during that year." The study also reported that an estimate of 24.4% of males had experienced minor IPV and 7.6% had experienced "severe assault."[146] "What is striking, is that the prevalence of exposure to violence is already high among young women aged 15–19 years, suggesting that violence commonly starts early in women's relationships,"[147] so imagine what the number is of males that are

---

[144] California Partnership to End Domestic Violence (2012). Cpedv.org.

[145] Vagi, K. J., O'Malley Olson, E., Basile, K. C., & Vivolo-Kantor, (2015). Teen dating violence (physical and sexual) among US high school students: Findings from the 2013 national youth risk behavior survey. JAMA Pediatrics, 169(5), 474-482.

[146] Straus, Murray A. (March 2008). *"Dominance and symmetry in partner violence by male and female university students in 32 nations" (PDF)*. Children and Youth Services Review. **30** (3): 258. doi:*10.1016/j.childyouth.2007.10.004*.

[147] (WHO United Nations, London School of Hygiene & Tropical Medicine, South African Medical Research Council, 2013)

exposed to violence who are between the ages of 15-19 years of age. "One in three girls in the US is a victim of physical, emotional or verbal abuse from a dating partner, a figure that far exceeds rates of other types of youth violence."[148]

For instance, when a female becomes pregnant, many authorities in the research field of domestic violence feel that domestic violence intensifies during pregnancy, which often leads to complications of pregnancy an issue which is significantly higher for abused women. "Each year, approximately 1.5 million women in the United States report a rape or physical assault by an intimate partner. This number includes as many as 324,000 women who are pregnant when violence occurs."[149] "Violence during pregnancy has been associated with: miscarriage; late entry into prenatal care; stillbirth; premature labor and birth; fetal injury; and low-birth-weight or small-for-gestational age infants."[165]

Some of the other challenges that teenagers face from a behavioral perspective are experiencing school failure because in some cases they are absent all of the time. Many of these teens are also dealing with or personally experiencing substance abuse, parentification, they become a runaway, they become incorrigible by acting out or becoming violent, they begin lying to avoid confrontation, they begin having rigid defenses, they become manipulative, they begin experiencing bouts of dependency, and they begin having mood swings.[166] Additional challenges that teenagers face both emotionally and psychologically are, grief, depression, suicide ideation, shame, guilt,

---

[148] (Love is Respect, 2014)

[149] (Division of Reproductive Health, National Center for Chronic Disease Prevention and Health Promotion, 2013) [165] (Pan American Health Organization - World Health Organization 2012) [166] California Partnership to End Domestic Violence (2012). Cpedv.org.

and self-blame, they too experience confusion about conflicting feeling towards their parents, they have anger issues and display signs of embarrassment.[150]

Now when speaking about healthy relationships, some of the characteristics of a healthy relationship is that both partners talk about their feelings. It is important that they each respect partner's friends and activities, it is also important that they consider the other person's opinions and feelings, respect each other's differences, have equal say in the relationship and find solutions to disagreements that work for both partners.[151] Some of the developmental assets for teens and knowing that they too are resilient, is by allowing them to demonstrate that they have the ability overcome teen domestic violence with support empowerment groups and having positive individuals around them, and by knowing what their boundaries and expectations are. Additional assets are by assisting them on how to be wise and constructively use their time as they begin learning how to advocate for themselves. We also need to show teens that they are learning how to make a commitment to their learning, by recognizing unhealthy relationships and by having positive values with someone such as an adult to assist them with working through their problems.[152]

Some of the short-term effect is that many researchers have adjusted the protocol recruitment strategies, data collection procedures, measures, and program administration, and eliminated the follow-up calls from the health educator. They also determined that the intervention that was being provided was actually reaching the high-risk groups of teens who had been exposed to an average of seven years of domestic

[150] California Partnership to End Domestic Violence (2012). Cpedv.org.
[151] California Partnership to End Domestic Violence (2012). Cpedv.org.
[152] California Partnership to End Domestic Violence (2012). Cpedv.org.

violence and had high rates of dating violence compared with national averages. These teens also had high rates of exposure to bullying, sexual harassment, and peer aggression, as both victims and perpetrators.

Overall, the mothers and youth who were participants of this program reported that they enjoyed the booklets and found them helpful and informative. However, when asked more in depth about the booklets, researchers were actually given low rates about the booklet completion and follow-ups, demonstrating that the researchers could not decisively determine what effects the booklets actually had. The pilot study was instrumental in guiding the development, refinement, and implementation of a larger, ongoing efficacy trial of the intervention that is being funded by the Centers for Disease Control and Prevention (CDC).[153] For more information, here are some resources for teen who are experiences problems with domestic abuse through dating.

Love is Respect www.loveisrespect.org

Offer 24-hour support regarding teen dating abuse.

Teens can call 1-866-331-9474 or go to the website for live chat.

Break the Cycle www.breakthecycle.org

California Youth Crisis Line www.youthcrisisline.org

Offer 24-hour support to youth in crisis.

Teens can call 1-800-843-5200 or go to the website for live chat.

---

[153] Read the final technical report *Dating Abuse Prevention in Teens of Moms with Domestic Violence Protection Orders (pdf, 405 pages)*. Learn more about the *CDC's Randomized Efficacy Trial of Moms and Teens for Safe Dates*.

California Partnership to End Domestic Violence

Strengthening Capacity for Prevention

http://www.cpedv.org/overview/strengthening-capacity-prevention

Prevention Policy http://www.cpedv.org/general-information/prevention-policy

Chapter 6

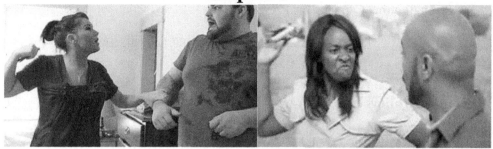

The Batterer: She Gave Him the Princess's Upper Cut!

According to societal attitudes, women are expected to be more naturally nurturing, compassionate, and understanding, however, society should not negate the facts that there are some women who are most definitely violent, more so than men. In the United States, there are several men's rights websites, which claims that there is "a vast prevalence of battering of men by women, at least equal to the rate and severity of the victimization of women."[154] If domestic violence is viewed from an analytical perspective demonstrating that males are also victims of domestic violence, then this would mean that females can also be perpetrators as well. With that being said, domestic violence now cannot be just a viewed as a feminist issue only.

Much of the research that is conducted as of today concerning male victims of domestic violence does not even contemplate asking the question of whether or not males are even victims, and when such a question is asked, how common is the question that is being asked? The reason why society has such negative attitudes about asking such questions concerning males being victims of domestic violence is partly

---

[154] The internet offers a huge number of websites on domestic violence, some of which include material on men as victims. See <www.blainn.cc/abuse, www.safe4all.org>, as well as sites devoted specifically to the issue of 'battered men' (<www.vix.com/menmag> and <www.vix.com/pub/men>).

attributable to the fact that domestic violence research for females is backed up more by the fact that there is a crisis services. So, when you read between the lines, the lack of asking such questions means that it is more important for the females to receive help and not as important for the males to receive help. Because domestic violence against males is so underreported, the subject does not appear to meet a significant need for those males who are victim of domestic violence for support. This is why real men suffer too.

Official records indicate that there are many females who are more apt to seek help being victims of domestic violence than males. Reason being is because male victims are less likely than female victims to report their abuse to the police or hospital. National crime and personal safety surveys can be carried out in different ways. The general picture produced from overseas sources is one where, while overall men are more often victims of violent crime, than intimate violence (which tends to include same-sex relationships and former partners) it is both more common and more likely to result in injury for women than it is for men.[155]

Because the statistical data is so limited concerning male victims of domestic violence, it was noticed that there were some interesting differences among ethnic groups. For instance, "women's risk of victimization over a 12-month period in Britain did not appear to vary significantly according to ethnicity, but Bangladeshi/Pakistani men were much less likely than white men to say that they had been assaulted by a partner.[156] White men were the only men whose self-reports of victimization actually

---

[155] For example, Dobash et al 1992: 74-76, Bachman 1994, Craven 1996, Mirrlees-Black 1999, Rennison and Welchans 2000
[156] Mirrlees-Black, Catriona (1999), Domestic Violence: Findings from a new British crime survey self-completion questionnaire, Home Office, London

slightly (but not statistically significantly) outnumbered those of women from the same racial category.[157] The report gives no cross-analysis between issues like self-blame and ethnic group.[158]

Exactly where is the outrage when males are hurt, harmed, or killed as a result of domestic violence? Everyone stays silent, why, is it because of the stereotypical stigmas and biases that says that men are supposed to suck it up and take the beating like a man or is it that omitting or limiting such information from statistical research says that it is okay to harm males. Just this statement alone should bring about awareness to society that society is promoting violence. No one should be hurt, harmed, or killed as a result of domestic violence. Domestic violence and double standards against men who are true victims of domestic violence is where men get shackles and women get chuckles. And this is the hidden stories of why males suffer in silence.

If we look beyond the self-defense, we will see that studies have found that there are a range of causes for female perpetrated IPV. What many in society do not know is that there are 1 in 4 men who have been physically abused (slapped, pushed, shoved) by an intimate partner.[159] "1 in 7 men have been severely physically abused (hit with a fist or hard object, kicked, slammed against something, choked, burned, etc.) by an intimate

---

[157] It is not exactly clear from any of the statistical reports on how many relationships were cross-cultural, and how ethnicity and same-sex relationships inter-related.

[158] Part of the problem with some of the analytical data is that the base concerning the male population is already a small proportion of the total number of respondents, so even in a large survey which often tries to compensate for such skewed data, then becomes an even smaller measurement with relevance. The survey methods are still likely to underestimate the 'true' amount of violence anyway (see e.g. the discussion of others' presence during respondents' completion of the survey – Mirrlees- Black 1999: 96-99). Percentages within percentages like 'victims who blamed themselves' must then be calculated. Even when available, results may therefore not be regarded as statistically significant. This supports the case for research to concentrate on 'minority' groups as the study population, providing the methods are seen as appropriate and necessary by those communities.

[159] Black, M.C., Basile, K.C., Breiding, M.J., Smith, S.G., Walters, M.L., Merrick, M.T., Chen, J. & Stevens, M. (2011). The national intimate partner and sexual violence survey: 2010 summary report. Retrieved from http://www.cdc.gov/violenceprevention/pdf/nisvs_report2010-a.pdf.

partner at some point in their lifetime."[160] "Nearly 1 in 10 men in the United States has experienced rape, physical violence, and/or stalking by an intimate partner and reported at least one measured impact related to experiencing these or other forms of violent behavior in the relationship (e.g., being fearful, concerned for safety, post-traumatic stress disorder (PTSD) symptoms, need for healthcare, injury, contacting a crisis hotline, need for housing services, need for victim's advocate services, need for legal services, missed at least one day of work or school)."[178] "1 in 18 men are severely injured by intimate partners in their lifetimes."[161] "Male rape victims and male victims of non-contact unwanted sexual experiences reported predominantly male perpetrators. Nearly half of stalking victimizations against males were also perpetrated by males. Perpetrators of other forms of violence against males were mostly female."[162]

Females such as Kelly Brook, Hope Solo, Carmen Electra, and Pamela Anderson are just a few of many female aggressors that were involved in domestic violence relationships. Now even though there are 1 in 4 females who are victims of domestic violence and 1 in 7 males that are also victims of domestic violence, there are 1 in 4 females who have openly admitted that they are the abuser.

In 1978 an author by the name of Suzanne Steinmetz wrote a scholarly article titled, "The Battered Husband Syndrome," which was published in Victimology: An International Journal. In Steinmetz's article she speaks about "how husband abuse was

[160] Ibid.

[178] Ibid.

[161] Black, M. C., Basile, K. C., Breiding, M. J., Smith, S. G., Walters, M. L., Merrick, M. T., Chen, J. & Stevens, M. (2011). The national intimate partner and sexual violence survey: 2010 summary report. Retrieved from http://www.cdc.gov/violenceprevention/pdf/nisvs_report2010-a.pdf.

[162] Black, M.C., Basile, K.C., Breiding, M.J., Smith, S.G., Walters, M.L., Merrick, M.T., Chen, J. & Stevens, M. (2011). The national intimate partner and sexual violence survey: 2010 summary report. Retrieved from http://www.cdc.gov/violenceprevention/pdf/nisvs_report2010-a.pdf.

not uncommon, although many tend to ignore it, dismiss it, or treated it with "selective inattentiveness." The reasons why men do not report their victimization and why they stay in an abusive situation are examined in depth. Some of the myths commonly held about men's place in the family, their attachment to their offspring and their ability to easily move in and out of relationships are exploded."

After the publishing of her article, Steinmetz stated that she began receiving verbal threats and anonymous phone calls from radical women's groups. She went on to say that "she found it ironic that the same people who claimed that women-initiated violence is purely in self-defense of their denials and are so quick to threaten people who do nothing more than threaten a scientific study." This was recognized in 1978 and was obviously recognized by others before that but they were blacklisted for sharing such information. Since this is a patriarchal society, research done on male victims of domestic violence is very limited because of a lack of funding and because real men don't tell. Data is also limited because mainstream society only hears half the truth. The reason why such information is contradictory and rarely discussed is because women's groups have sympathetic politicians and the judicial system in their corner as they use their power to suppress the truth.

Societal attitudes are that males who are victims of domestic violence are weak cowards, yet we know that this is not true, and again, this is why males suffer in silence, because real men don't tell. Many men are being villainized for hitting women, but women who are known to abuse men are being praised and that is where the domestic violence double standards come in to play. Domestic violence, double standards, where women get praise for domestic abuse and men get sanctioned for domestic abuse.

In an article written in 2010 by Amanda Hass in the Washington City Paper she showed that there were 21 males who were killed as a result of domestic violence and that was just in the state of Maryland. In that same year, there were 32 females killed as a result of domestic violence in the same state. Even though this data is 8 years old, it is evident that more and more females are becoming more aggressive towards males. So why is it that more women are not always being held accountable for harming males or are ignored when they are recognized as the abuser? Is it because of societal attitudes and the social stigma says that men cannot be victims of domestic violence? Women should be held just as accountable for abusing men as men are for abusing women. No matter how the situation is viewed, domestic violence is wrong and has to stop. Male victims of domestic violence have been marginalized and systematically ignored, and this is due to many advocates and the media focusing exclusively on the female victims of domestic violence.

A study that was conducted by the National Coalition Against Domestic Violence showed that there were more than 835,732 males that were victims of domestic violence, yet those studies are rarely spoken of or are omitted from many studies. Understand that the NCADV is not the only offender that uses the same practices. There are more than 600 internet sites that quote the same things which is the reporting of half the story by omitting the statistics of males that are victims. As far as these sites are concerned, male victims of domestic violence simply do not exist and only their preferred halves are quoted. Double standards, domestic violence, this is the hidden story and why males suffer in silence.

The unveiling or exposing of female perpetrators of domestic violence began in

1980 when Murray Straus, Richard Gelles and Suzanne Steinmetz, published a comparative study on the topic in the United States. All three researchers were considered to be an update with their information, especially in the feminist circles, as being experts in the field of "spousal abuse." In all their previous studies Straus and his colleagues had assumed that battered husbands were a rare occurrence and, in any case, would not be seriously injured. In the 1980 study, there was a more thorough investigation of these assumptions that was undertaken when the team noted the absence of evidence that underlies these assumptions in the more than 30 works comprising the body of knowledge at that point. These researchers came to the surprising conclusion that, overall, 11.6 percent of women, but 12 percent of the men had stated they had been beaten, slapped, kicked, bitten, pelted with objects or to have been otherwise attacked. (Some studies showed that the "physical force" on the preconceived notion, even came to 25 percent of attacked men compared with 16.5 percent of women.)

For each 1.8 million female victims there are two million male victims. If a woman was attacked, which would be for each 17.5 seconds, then every 15.7 seconds there was a man who would be attacked. This concealment of relevant information, as Murray Straus noted, "promotes some annoying questions about scientific ethics to light." After a renewed, yet thorough examination was conducted of the data, Straus and his colleagues concluded: That in a quarter of the cases where domestic violence was committed, the violence was committed by the man, while half of all the other cases were exclusively by the woman, with the balance involving both genders without a specified sequence.

Once this new information surfaced, the representatives of the women's movement were suddenly not so happy with their former idols. The feminist assumption as it had been known was being threatened and beginning to falter. Today, many researchers in the field of domestic violence have now attempted studies of their own to prove that the study by Straus, Gelles and Steinmetz was a single deviation, however, many of these researchers had to realize that even their own results confirmed Straus, Gelles and Steinmetz's original findings. Some of these studies even showed even more dramatic results: for example, American females that were high school students were four times as likely as male students to be the only violator against a member of the other gender participant of the event reported (5.7 %: 1.4 %).

A study that was conducted in New Zealand found that women and men committed slight violence against the opposite sex in the ratio of 22 to 36 percent, severe violence even in the ratio of 6 to 19 percent. Straus also interviewed women in shelters who had sought refuge. Again, Straus found that about half of them had attacked their partners on their own. Straus was ignored from then by the feminist fighting literature,[163] that had been quoted from earlier. Likewise, he found himself exposed to personal attacks and slander. It was also stated that even the chairman of the "Canadian Association of Violence against Women," Pat Marshall, began spreading the rumor that Straus would mistreat his own wife, for which she later recanted and apologized to him only after repeated requests. Even fiercer treatment was given to Suzanne Steinmetz, the woman in Straus' research group: She received bomb threats,

---

[163] It is noteworthy that in Wikipedia only Richard James Gelles has an article and in the article Conflict tactics scale is explained in an extensive paragraph, why Murray is wrong.

and her children were told they were targeted by fanatics. Apparently without any awareness of the contradictions inherent in their actions, the supporters of feminist ideologies of violence attacked us to enforce their view that women are far less violent than men.[164]

A study that was conducted in Canada showed that between "2000 and 2009, there were 738 spousal homicides, accounting for nearly half (47%) of all solved family homicides. These included current and former legally married spouses and common law spouses aged 15 years and over. The perpetrators were predominantly male (n= 585, 79%) vs. female (n= 153, 21%). The rate of spousal homicide against women was about three times higher than that against men. Stabbing was the most common method used to commit spousal homicide, particularly against male victims. Male victims were more likely to be killed by a common law partner (66%), while women were slightly more likely to be killed by their legally married spouse (39%) than by a common law partner (33%). Male victims (11%) were less likely than female victims (26%) to be killed by a partner from whom they were separated or divorced. For both male and female spouses, rates peaked among 15- to 24-year-olds and declined with increasing age (Statistics Canada, 2009). A review of the literature reveals that despite much research on spousal homicide, few studies have addressed spousal homicides committed by women.[165]

The use of domestic violence against men as a tool of humor is offensive and very inappropriate. Again, this is why males suffer in silence. It causes these men not to seek help, and worse, oftentimes abandon their family to get away from the abuser, leaving

---

[164] Arne Hoffmann: Häusliche Gewaltist weiblich, Novo-Magazine 45, March/April 2000
[165] Correspondence to: Dominique Bourget, M.D., Forensic Psychiatry and Schizophrenia Programs, Royal Ottawa Mental Health Centre, 1145 Carling Avenue, Ottawa, Ontario K1Z 7K4, Canada. E-mail: dominiquebourget@gmail.com

their children behind to become the probable next target. Women who abuse men are not much different than their male counterparts. When male victims are ignored then so are their children and then those children become damaged because they must continually witness the abuse. "Females are more likely to be killed by an intimate partner than in any other type of relationship. For instance, among U.S. female homicide victims, roughly one in three is killed by an intimate partner, whereas among male homicide victims, only one in twenty are killed by an intimate partner. Moreover, the proportion of female homicide victims killed by an intimate partner has gradually increased from 1989 to 2001."[166] "Among U. S. homicides, the intimate partner is the only victim offender relationship category where female-perpetrated homicide rates approach that of men."[167] Based on research examining the sex ratio of spousal killings, roughly 60 to 70. American females kill an intimate partner for every 100 males that do so."[168]

When it came to deciphering statistics concerning domestic violence there were some research data bases that were racially disaggregated the SPOK becomes exceptionally high for Black females at an astonishing 92 (Gauthier & Bankston, 2004). When females kill, they are more likely to kill someone that is close to them, such as an intimate partner or a family member, making the intimate partner the only victim offender relationship where female perpetration reaches levels similar to males (Browne

[166] KEHNSMITH AND KERNSMITH. "*Treating Female Perpetrators: State Standards for Batterer Intervention Services.*" Social Work VOLUME 54, NUMBER 4 OCTOBER 2009.
[167] Browne, Williams, & Dutton, 1999
[168] (Gauthier & Bankston, 1997; Gauthier & Bankston, 2004; Wilson & Daly, 1992).

et al., 1999). Research has also shown that females kill intimate partners for different reasons than males who kill their intimate partners (Saunders, 2002).[169]

For informational purposes, disaggregated means, to separate into component parts. However, for the purposes of this book, we are focusing on disaggregated data which refers to numerical or non-numerical information that has been (1) collected from multiple sources and/or on multiple measures, variables, or individuals; (2) compiled into **aggregate data**—i.e., summaries of data—typically for the purposes of public reporting or statistical analysis; and then (3) broken down in component parts or smaller units of data. For example, information about whether individual students graduated from high school can be compiled and summarized into a single graduation rate for a school or a graduating class, and annual graduation rates for individual schools can then be aggregated into graduation rates for districts, states, and countries. Graduation rates can then be *disaggregated* to show, for example, the percentage of male and female students, or white and non-white students, who graduated. Generally speaking, data is disaggregated for the purpose of revealing underlying trends, patterns, or insights that would not be observable in aggregated data sets, such as disparities in **standardized-test scores** or enrollment patterns across different categories of students, for example.[170]

While most disaggregated education data is numerical, it's both possible and common to disaggregate non-numeric information. For example, educators, students, and parents in a school district may be surveyed on a topic, and the information and

[169] KEHNSMITH AND KERNSMITH. *"Treating Female Perpetrators: State Standards for Batterer Intervention Services."* Social Work VOLUME 54, NUMBER 4 OCTOBER 2009.
[170] https://www.edglossary.org/**disaggregated-data**

comments from those surveys could then be aggregated into a report that shows what the three groups—educators, students, and parents—collectively think and feel about the issue. The compiled information could then be disaggregated and reported for each distinct group to compare differences in how educators, students, and parents perceive the issue. Information collected during polls, interviews, and focus groups can be aggregated and disaggregated in a similar fashion.[171]

To further illustrate the concept of disaggregated data and how it may be used in public education, consider a school with an enrollment of 500 students, which means the school maintains 500 student records, each of which contains a wide variety of information about the enrolled students—for example, first and last name, home address, date of birth, racial or ethnic identification, date and period of enrollment, courses taken and completed, course-grades earned, test scores, etc. (the information collected and maintained on individual students is often called **student-level data**, among other terms). Once or twice a year, the school district may be required to submit student-enrollment reports to their state department of education. Each school in the district will then compile a report that documents the number of students currently enrolled in the school and in each grade level, which requires administrators to summarize data from all their individual student records to produce the enrollment reports. The district now has *aggregate* enrollment information about the students attending its schools.

Over the next five years, the school district could use these annual reports to analyze increases or declines in district-wide enrollment, enrollment at each school, or

---

[171] https://www.edglossary.org/**disaggregated-data**

enrollment at each grade level. The district could not, however, determine whether there have been increases or declines in the enrollment of white and non-white students based on the aggregate data it received from its schools. To produce a report showing distinct enrollment trends for different races and ethnicities, for example, the district schools would then need to *disaggregate* the enrollment information by racial and ethnic subgroups.[172]

Even though domestic violence, historically, has been considered to be a crime that is primarily perpetrated by men, the data from statistical research shows that there has been an increase in the number of women who are being arrested and mandated into batterer intervention programs compared to 40 years ago. Because such studies has been constantly researched, there are now existing state policies that have begun to explore the degree to which these statistics address the unique needs of including women into batterer intervention programs.[173] In approximately states, 30 percent of all the people that arrested for domestic violence are female (Klein, 2001}, with the national average being nearly 20 percent (Duróse et al., 2005).[174] Research further indicates that women, particularly adolescents, are perpetrating more violence than they had in the past. So now, the arrest rates for female adolescents have grown at more than twice the pace of the rates for male adolescents since 1989 (U.S. Department of justice, 1996).

[172] https://www.edglossary.org/**disaggregated-data**

[173] KEHNSMITH AND KERNSMITH. *"Treating Female Perpetrators: State Standards for Batterer Intervention Services."* Social Work VOLUME 54, NUMBER 4 OCTOBER 2009.

[174] KEHNSMITH AND KERNSMITH. *"Treating Female Perpetrators: State Standards for Batterer Intervention Services."* Social Work VOLUME 54, NUMBER 4 OCTOBER 2009.

Although women account for 18 percent of aggravated assault arrests, arrests of women for violent crimes have increased by 55 percent, compared with 33 percent for men. If this trend continues, it is likely that rates of female perpetrated domestic violence will increase.[175] Some national studies have indicated that women are just as likely as men to behave aggressively in intimate relationships.[176] Although female perpetrators represent a minority of domestic violence arrests, a large number of women are arrested and mandated into programs.[177]

In their early stages of research, the domestic violence theories and practices were based on the assumption that men were the perpetrators and women were the victims. Feminist theories, as summarized by McCall and Shields (1986), are based on the assumption that domestic violence results from patriarchal social structures. Although an important consideration for male-on female violence, this theory appears to provide little information on the nature of female-perpetrated violence given that the gendered power imbalance should serve to deter this type of violence.[178]
Even today, it seems as though the majority of research that is conducted is only examining the effectiveness of batterer treatment programs which still continues to focus exclusively on the male's use of violence. The problem with this analogy is that this further exacerbates the problem that society, research and funding are not providing

---

[175] KEHNSMITH AND KERNSMITH. *"Treating Female Perpetrators: State Standards for Batterer Intervention Services."* Social Work VOLUME 54, NUMBER 4 OCTOBER 2009.

[176] KEHNSMITH AND KERNSMITH. *"Treating Female Perpetrators: State Standards for Batterer Intervention Services."* Social Work VOLUME 54, NUMBER 4 OCTOBER 2009. (O'Leary et al., 1989; Straus, Gelles, & Steinmetz. 19H0; Vivian & Langhinrichsen-Rohling, 1994)

[177] KEHNSMITH AND KERNSMITH. *"Treating Female Perpetrators: State Standards for Batterer Intervention Services."* Social Work VOLUME 54, NUMBER 4 OCTOBER 2009.

[178] KEHNSMITH AND KERNSMITH. *"Treating Female Perpetrators: State Standards for Batterer Intervention Services."* Social Work VOLUME 54, NUMBER 4 OCTOBER 2009.

services to female perpetrators. It is not whether or not the theories and models that guides such practices are appropriate for women, because the outcomes of these interventions have yet to be examined. It is also suggested that it is about high time that the judicial system as well as the media begins to focus on the fact that domestic violence against men does exist and should be thoroughly researched.

Facts are that the violence that is perpetrated by women has risen steeply in the last half of the century. Could it be that 'women's liberation' are beginning to abuse their power and authority or is it really just some females showing their ability to have a natural killer instinct? When it is thought of this way, I look at the 1956 version of the 'Bad Seed.' Because of societal stigmas, many men are not so inclined to find it amusing when the "little woman" lashes out at them, belts them with an upper cut while many chuckle and approve the violence. There was one survey of college students that showed that there were 20 percent of men who had been physically attacked by their current and past girlfriends, and they did not think that such physical violence was funny. Many of the abusive behaviors and characteristics of an abuser are, that abusers are not discriminatory in the sense that they do come in all races, ethnicities, cultures, professions, socioeconomic classes, educational backgrounds, and all physical sizes.

Some of the other characteristics of an abuser is that the abuser can have self-esteem issues (may be too low or too high), the abuser believes in a "traditional" patriarchal family structure with a dominant male as head of the household, the abuser will blame others for their actions or inactions, the abuser is pathologically jealous and the abuser believes that their violent behavior is justified and does not need to be punished. The abuser will have a need for absolute control, the abuser will fear being alone, the abuser will appear to lack guilt, shame and remorse over their actions, the abuser may also have or hide a lot of guilt, shame and remorse over their actions, the abuser will also deny allegations of abuse or become hostile when confronted, the abuser will become manipulative, when in public or around others, the abuser will become socially charming. What we need to know about the behavior of an abuser is that an abusive behavior is a learned behavior, but it can also be unlearned. Abuse is not about anger, we must understand that the abusers are not out of control—they are, in fact, in absolute control. There are batterer intervention programs that can help the batterer unlearn these negative behaviors. Such programs are designed for individuals who have been arrested for domestic violence which may consist of educational classes, treatment groups, evaluations, individual counseling, and case management.

What we do know is that today there are many male survivors of domestic violence who have begun to speak out about their own experiences who will argue that, just like female victims who are survivor's domestic violence, they too deserve to be heard and believed rather than being marginalized if not downright ignored. Society must understand that just because a male is a victim of domestic violence does not mean that he is anti-feminist, many men indeed who work in the area of domestic violence are actively pro-feminist in their understanding and activism.

Research conducted by Linda Gordon and her "historical case studies show how in one family a woman could be both victimized by her husband and then turns around and abuses her own children. The manipulation aspect that now comes into play will be how the victim/perpetrator in her dealings with welfare and social workers, could by the same token be subjected to forces that are beyond her control and manage to manipulate the situation in order achieve some type of desirable outcomes for herself."[179] Gordon's research also brought up salient characteristics that when it comes to the harsh reality of domestic violence, it is possible and common that a woman can be both the victim and the perpetrator. She can also in turn be abusive to the person that is abusing her, so to view her as being powerless or powerful really does not justify such a complex situation when it comes to being violent.

In recent years, abused husbands and boyfriends have gained increased attention. More men than women have become victims of intimate partner physical violence within the past year, according to a national study funded by the Centers for Disease Control and U.S. Department of Justice. According to the National Intimate Partner and Sexual Violence Survey (hereinafter NISVS) released in December 2011, that in 2010 an estimated 5,365,000 men and 4,741,000 women were victims of intimate partner physical violence.[180] These findings contrasted to earlier reports from National Violence Against Women Survey[181] (hereinafter NVAWS), which estimated that 1.2 million women and 835,000 men were victims of intimate partner physical violence during those preceding 12 months. (One-year prevalence "are considered to be more accurate [than lifetime rates] because they do not depend on recall of events long past."[182]

There are thousands of support programs, web sites and public-interest media for female victims of domestic violence, yet there are virtually no programs for males and only a handful of web sites for male victims. Maybe this is because males, but not

---

[179] Gordon, Linda (1988), Heroes of their Own Lives: The politics and history of family violence, Boston 1880-1960, Viking, New York
[180] Black, M.C. et al., 2011, Tables 4.1 and 4.2.
[181] Tjaden, P. G., & Thoennes, N., 2000
[182] Straus, 2005, p. 60

females, have gotten the message that domestic violence is wrong. Now, to debunk the gender bias aspect, society has many programs for men who stand up against domestic violence by men, yet they have no programs that urge women to stand up against domestic violence by women. Something to think about. "Studies show that men are less likely than women to seek help, and those that do have to overcome internal and external hurdles."[183]

There has been little research or responses concerning male victims of intimate partner violence, mostly because there are so many agencies that refuses to fund such research. "In the few studies done, many men report that hotline workers say they only help women, imply or state the men must be the instigators, ridicule them or refer them to batterers' programs. Police often will fail to respond, ridicule the man or arrest him."[184] In 2008 Douglas and Hines conducted the first-ever large-scale national survey of men who sought help for heterosexual physical intimate partner violence.[185] In this national survey there were approximately 302 men were surveyed. This study found that between half and two-thirds of the men who contacted the police, a DV agency, or a DV hotline reported that these resources were "not at all helpful."[186] The study conducted in 2008 by Douglas and Hines elaborated that on a large proportion of male victims of domestic violence who sought help from DV agencies (49.9%), DV hotlines (63.9%), or online resources (42.9%) were told, "We only help women."[205] Of the 132 men who sought help from a DV agency, 44.1% (n=86) said that none of these resource were not

---

[183] Galdas et al., 2005, and Cook 2009.
[184] Cook 2009, and Douglas and Hines, 2011.
[185] Douglas and Hines, 2011
[186] Cook 2009, and Douglas and Hines, 2011.
[205]

at all helpful; the study went on to further state that 95.3% of those men (n=81) said that they were given the impression that the agency was being biased against men.. Some of the men were accused of being the batterer in the relationship: This happened to men seeking help from DV agencies (40.2%), DV hotlines (32.2%) and online resources (18.9%). Over 25% of those using an online resource reported that they were given a phone number for help which turned out to be the number for a batterer's program. The results from the open-ended questions showed that 16.4% of the men who contacted a hotline reported that the staff made fun them, as did 15.2% of the men who contacted local DV agencies."[187]

Studies that were conducted concerning the response of the police showed that they arrested the male just as often as the violent partner (33.3% vs. 26.5%). The partner was deemed the "primary aggressor" in 54.9% of the cases. In 41.5% of the cases where the men called the police, the police usually asked whether or not he wanted his partner arrested; in 21% of these cases, the police refused to arrest the partner, and in 38.7% the police made reference that there was nothing they could do and left. Studies also showed that there were some 68% of the men who began turning to mental health professionals.

In some cases, the male victim said that those professionals would take their concerns seriously, but only 30.1% of those same professionals offered information on how male victims of domestic violence could get help from a DV program. Although there were 106 men who suffered severe physical injury, there were only 54 who actually sought help from a medical provider. When some of them which were 90.1% were asked how they received their injuries, only 60.4% answered truthfully, yet only 14% were able

---

[187] Douglas and Hines, 2011, page 7

to obtain the information that they needed in getting help from a program for intimate partner violence.[188]

The best source that a male victim of domestic violence can go to for help is friends, neighbors, relatives, lawyers, ministers and the like. Again, studies indicated that approximately 84.9% male victims of domestic violence turned to one or more of these sources, and 90% of those victims found these resources to be helpful. Two-thirds of the male victims who sought online help and support, with half the men surveyed using Web sites and a quarter using an online support group. Some 69.1% found online support helpful; 44.9% used a resource for male victims and 42.6% for anyone experiencing partner aggression.[208] Remember, men of domestic violence, and double standards causes male victims to again be victimized.

What we must do to bring awareness to the public about male domestic violence is to recognize that there is intimate partner violence by women, we must understand it, and recognize it as a serious social problem. We must promote more public service announcements and address that there is a need for these announcements to be neutral gender biased. As it currently stands, such promotions mainly focus almost exclusively on intimate partner violence against women. There needs to be more public education about violence to men.

There are many websites on intimate partner violence against women, but unfortunately for the male victims of domestic violence, these are all woman-centered websites, or they use gender-neutral language. These sites tend to minimize the violence that is committed against men. There are only a handful of sites that addresses the issue

---

[188] , pp 7 & 8

domestic violence against men. We must also understand and keep in mind that there is no one that is gender immune to violence and psychological manipulation. This culture concerning the victim's abuse needs a full shift in perspective, because abuse is abuse, and a victim is a victim. Abuse should not be tolerated under any circumstances. Today, the toll of abuse on both men and women has become enormous.

For anyone who is abused they should be given the opportunity to get help and should be able to do so in an environment that is not shameful or accusatory. Again, men who are victims of domestic violence must be encouraged to get help as well. Men usually have many of the same signs of abuse as women do. They like women have behavioral changes, they show signs of isolation as when around crowds they will suddenly disappear from social circles, and they are not willing to talk about it what is going on. Because woman-on-man violence is often turned into onscreen amusement, men will withdraw even more. The violence that is done to them is not taken seriously but more like on a reality show with the punch line being more of a larger and depressing narrative.[189]

When it comes to male victims of domestic violence and reality dramatics, Anne P. Mitchell "points to the case of John and Lorena Bobbitt, which made national news in 1993 when Lorena cut off her husband's penis. This aftermath ended up turning into a circus. Mitchell says the initial response of many radio and talk shows was just to laugh at the incident. "If something remotely similar had happened to a woman, there would have been a very different response," Mitchell tells Yahoo Health.[190] In the case of

---

[189] Anne P. Mitchell, a retired professor of family law at Lincoln Law School of San Jose (Calif.) and one of the first fathers'-rights lawyers in the country.
[190] Anne P. Mitchell, a retired professor of family law at Lincoln Law School of San Jose (Calif.) and one of the first fathers'-rights lawyers in the country.

Bobbitt the male verses Bobbitt the female, she gave him the Princess Cut. Mitchell goes on to say that "based on old stereotypes and typical gender roles, it is often very difficult for men to get fair treatment. They are often stuck in situations in which they cannot win. "Many women who are aggressive toward their partners know that if the police are called out, they will arrest the man," she explains. "I once had a client, who was the mildest guy ever. In no way would he have ever been violent — but his girlfriend was very volatile and a drug user. Once, she was trying to provoke him to hit her. When he wouldn't respond, she raked her fingernails across his face. He was standing there bleeding when the police arrived at the house. They still arrested him."

According to Ruth Glenn, executive director of the National Coalition Against Domestic Violence "the reason for abuse is the same for men and women: "It is all about maintaining power and control over a partner," she tells Yahoo Health. And because "we still live in a patriarchal society, and when it is domestic violence, you are looked at as weaker when you are the victim

Chapter 7

Real Men Who Suffer Too, Death by Design

Because of a deeply rooted guilt that she possessed concerning his death and the way in which he died began eating away at her inner being, especially now with it being the seven-year anniversary of his death. Rasheedah felt that she should confess about Andre's death. First, she wrote a manuscript giving a descriptive account about how Andre really died. Once Rasheedah she published the book, then two weeks later she contacted the news stations and other forms of media such as radio and television shows, new paper and magazine outlets and directed letters to them to ask for forgiveness from Andre's family and friends. Rasheedah made the poor assumption that if she did this publicly, then people would have sympathy for her. In addition to Rasheedah submitting a copy of the book to these platforms concerning Andre's murder, she said that she just had to get it off of her chest, because as she had gone into her new marriage and did not want this cloud hanging over her. She imagined having another child with Andre and being with him once more every time she was intimate with her new husband. It was the guilt eating away at her, especially since her new husband favored Andre.

When Rasheedah wrote her book, she wrote it under a pen name as not to immediately raise suspicion to anyone, not even to her own family and friends, but especially to Andre's family and his friends. What would they think of her now that her book has been released, and the truth has been revealed? There was now going to be a movie made based on her book. She felt that she had to tell now. Would they accept and still love her? Would they ostracize her and turn her in to the law, or even FBI since she had since moved out of the state. What would happen now?

In Rasheedah's book, she admitted that she was an abuser. She also mentioned how she would punch, kick, scratch, pull Andre's hair and hit him with objects such as vases or whatever was closest to her. She also admitted how she would throw things at him. At one point, she even admitted to pulling a knife out on him and stabbing him in his upper arm. He was stabbed in a place where it was barely noticeable closer to his shoulder blade. The only reason why there was a concern about the cut, is because shortly after Andre was cut, he ended up falling down a flight of stairs as he was leaving some friends apartment. The wound became infected because he did not want to go to the hospital and admit that his wife, out of anger and a fit of rage had stabbed him and refused to let him go by himself so that he would not implicate her with the stabbing.

Andre's falling down the stairs caused great concern to his friends, and by him falling, he had apparently opened his wound which had been stitched up by Rasheedah, as she was in the army and learned how to stitch people up, including herself. Andre ended up staying in the hospital for a few weeks. Because infection had set in from the wound and Andre had a concussion, the doctors wanted to keep him under observation in hopes that he would confess the truth to what happened since his friends had already shared. Unfortunately, Andre had no intentions of revealing that information because he was in fear for his life. Rasheedah was at the hospital every day and half the night. And when she wasn't at the hospital, then she would call or have one of her male associates to sit with him, just to keep an eye on him. Andre was ordered to stay home from work, placed on bedrest for two months and was also placed in a program that sent a therapist and a nurse out to the home three times a week. The therapist came out twice a week and the nurse three times a week. He also had to complete one year of therapy.

While in the hospital, for some reason or another, when nurses weren't around, Andre kept falling in the hospital, he sustained bruises and ended up wheelchair bound, and for how long, who knew. Andre did not want this and mentioned to the doctors that he would be able to prove how independent he had become during his hospital stay. This was only said to prevent any more abuse towards him by Rasheedah and her goons.

During one of her home visits, Andre's assigned a nurse found out that he had again been pushed down the stairs at home after the first initial fall, since his visit at his friend's apartment. One of Andre's children was talking to the nurse about the progress of his recovery, and it just so happen to slip out about how as Rasheedah was pushing the wheelchair, how it seemed to have gotten caught on an area rug causing it to lean forward making him fall again. It was also confirmed by the nurse that Rasheedah had been involved because Rasheedah said that when the therapist left one day, Andre tried getting out of bed by himself and by some miraculous reason, made his way to the top of the stairs, without using the elevator and apparently lost his balance, falling down the stairs. Rasheedah's story was totally different than what their child said, raising the nurse's suspicions. Out of concern and elaborating on the matter, according to the therapist, Andre was depressed and had no desire to get out of bed. The nurse and therapist compared notes, once away from the home and it appeared that the most current fall was made to look like an accident which had now caused Andre to lose the feeling in the lower part of his body and become wheelchair bound a little longer than he anticipated.

Andre had high hopes of going back to work and getting back into his routine as he was becoming uncomfortable being at home around Rasheedah for long periods of time. One day during the therapist visit, he notices that Rasheedah had a habit of pushing Andre's wheelchair and tilting it forward which also caused him to fall, as if this was being done purposely. On this same day, the therapist happened to see the nurse pull up and did not let on to Rasheedah of what he observed. He went outside to meet with the nurse and give her an update about the progress of Andre's treatment and let her know to be safe as he was going back to the office to work on case notes and contact both child family services and adult protective services. The therapist also informs the nurse of what he witnessed and told her not to let on that she knew anything, again for both her safety and the safety of Andre and their children as he also noticed that there were some unsavory characters that had begun hanging around.

The nurse agreed that she would not let on what she was told, but she also wanted the therapist to make sure that he contacted Adult Protective Services right away so that they could do something to get Andre and his children out of the situation that he was in. Andre continued his façade of protecting Rasheedah, by always saying that it was an accident, or that he was accident prone and too lazy to use the elevator. At least this was the story that Andre shared with family and friends. It was as though Rasheedah was trying to end Andre's life for some reason or another. If she was so unhappy with him then why didn't she just leave him instead of trying to harm him? What did she have to gain?

Guess that Rasheedah's bad seed image was in her blood. Story has it that Rasheedah's biological mother had three of her husbands killed and almost got away with it. For years Rasheedah's mother thought that she was invincible, but one day 10 years later she began bragging and boasting about her evil deeds not realizing that she was in a public space and was not familiar with her audience. Someone happened to hear what she was saying and new the family of one of her husbands who met his unfortunate demise and informed law enforcement. She was eventually caught and extradited to the state where the death took place and prosecuted, being sentenced to death. Rasheedah's mother never did make it to the electric chair as she passed away less than a year of her being in prison under suspicious circumstances.

One day as the nurse was getting Andre dressed, she noticed that there was a wound on Andre's arm that was not properly healing. This was the wound that Rasheedah had bragged about in her book. When the nurse asked Andre what happened, he told her that the friend, whose flight of stairs that he fallen, which was due to his clumsiness, had come to take him out. He said that they had gone to a bar with some other of their friends, and someone began bullying him and talking about him being in the wheelchair. A fight ensued. He said that he was able to get a hold of the individual, and as he was getting the best of his bully, the bully then stabbed him in the shoulder with a knife.

The nurse told him that he should have reported the incident to the police, and then went to the hospital to get the wound treated as it was now infected. The nurse then told Andre that she would have to report the incident to her job and get a case manager involved concerning his condition as not to impede upon his current treatment, because the infection setting in and this was not good. The nursed asked

Andre what was the name of his friend so that she could corroborate his story to Andre's and add the information into her incident report.

As they were talking, Rasheedah had conveniently come home for lunch entering the house without being heard as though she were being sneaky having seen the nurse's car in the driveway. Rasheedah knew that the nurse would be at the house but for some reason she couldn't understand why the nurse would be parked in the driveway on this particular day. Rasheedah then carefully made her way up the stairs without making a sound. Rasheedah just happened to be standing near the door and purposely overheard the entire conversation about Andre being stabbed and about how he fell down his friends' stairs as a result of being clumsy. How did Rasheedah know exactly when to come home? How did she know that the nurse was going to be at the house at that particular time as she did not have a set schedule do to having other clients, and just as long as it was before 3:00 pm? How did Rasheedah know many of things that she knew? Did she have cameras put up or did she have the neighbors watching? Did she have someone following Andre? Relieved that Andre had not broken down and confided in the nurse about how he really fell down his friends' stairs, Rasheedah knew that she was in the clear for now. Andre on the other hand was blessed that he did not let on that Rasheedah was the real culprit or it could have all gone bad for both he and the nurse. Rasheedah then went back downstairs and quietly walked out of the door and then came in making noise as though she was actually coming in for the first time. As Rasheedah walked upstairs into the bedroom, Andre was telling the nurse that his friend did not want to get involved because he did not have a very good rapport with law enforcement.

The truth of the matter is that Rasheedah had originally been the one who pushed Andre down that flight of stairs as they were leaving his friends house causing him to fall becoming temporarily paralyzed. How long he would be paralyzed would be uncertain. But what was certain was that Rasheedah was the batterer and many of their close family and friends knew that she was the batterer because she had an aggressive behavior towards many of them, which included her own family.

Andre and Rasheedah met at the law firm where they worked as they were both attorneys. Andre was planning on leaving Rasheedah and getting full custody of the children as he had become tired of her and her abusive and manipulative behaviors. He also feared for their children's safety as she often lashed out at them in anger. Although Andre was in a wheelchair, and not knowing the future of his fate, it did not matter whether or not he would be wheelchair bound permanently, all that mattered to him was knowing that he and his children were safe, and he had to try and keep it that way. Andre knew that he had to get away from Rasheedah before something serious happened like him being killed the next time.

Rasheedah had once became so angry and enraged with Andre that she went upstairs, went into their wall safe, retrieved the small gun safe, took a gun out of that gun safe that was kept inside and opened fire inside of the house while the children were inside. Fortunately for her, because the both of them were very prominent people in the community, and of course were attorneys, Rasheedah told the police that she had taken the gun apart to clean it not realizing that a bullet was still in the chamber, and it accidentally went off. She was so good with fabricating the story that she told the police that they just gave her a warning. Rasheedah said that she was on the phone with a friend running off at the mouth and not paying attention to what she was doing, which is probably why she forgot to check the chamber. Once the police left, Rasheedah told

Andre that the only way that he would ever leave her would be over his dead body in a body bag before she would allow him to leave her and take their children.

Andre had slowly begun a routine and began going back to work. One night after Andre had come home from the office, Rasheedah had been drinking wine and was in a bad mood. Andre seeing this spoke as usual, keeping the conversation short, "how was your day at the office today," "Chrystal wanted me to tell you hey, said that she doesn't see you much anymore since you got your promotion and moved upstairs." "Honey, is everything alright?" "Well, since you're not in a mood to talk, then I'm going to head off to bed because it's been a long day for me with depositions and the new trainees. Rasheedah knowing that Andre had never cheated on her accused him of cheating on her and began an argument. Not wanting to wake the children up, Andre went to the closet, grabbed a pillow and a blanket, and went back downstairs to sleep on the couch. The couple had an elevator put inside of the house so that it would be easier for Andre to get up and down the stairs as she had left him alone at home a lot with the children refusing to hire an in-home care or a babysitter and he needed to be able to get to them without having to worry about getting up and down the stairs. Becoming so upset that Andre had gone downstairs to sleep on the couch, Rasheedah then ran downstairs into the kitchen, grabbed a knife and stabbed him in a fit of rage. That is how he got the wound in his shoulder.

A week later another incident happened where Andre just happened to fall out of his wheelchair when no one was around but he and Rasheedah. Rasheedah often tipped his wheelchair forward causing him to fall and sustain some type of injuries and one day she went too far killing him, again out of rage. This time it wasn't just a simple push of the wheelchair and oops you fall. On this particular Friday night, the children had gone over to Andre's family's house for a family function and were there to stay over the weekend. Andre and Rasheedah were to meet up with the children on the following Saturday. Rasheedah had made an elegant candlelight dinner which she rarely does. She purposely started an argument, knowing that Andre would not buy into what she was trying to do to and be baited, by Rasheedah's manipulation. She conveniently had some of her criminal associates, those whom she once represented, waiting in the room downstair where Andre had begun sleeping in while she went to the store closest by the office. This particular store, which happened to be miles away was used in order to establish her alibi as there were toll roads and cameras. After leaving the store, Rasheedah headed to Andre's family's home which was also in the opposite direction of their home as it was an eight-hour drive away. This allowed Rasheedah's associates to have enough time to brutally beat Andre, take him upstairs on the elevator and then pushed him down the stairs making it seem as though he had an accident in a wheelchair trying to run or wheel his chair from those attacking him. Then they shot him several times in the head making it seem as though it was a burglary gone wrong.

Rasheedah had been planning this for months knowing that Andre's family even was coming. Before Rasheedah left to execute her planned alibi, it was obvious that she had everything meticulously planned, as she made sure that everything was perfect to her expectations. She also had her so-called associates and hired killers to cut the wires to the surveillance cameras and short out some of the fuses. She then had rose petals spread out across on the bed, and on the floor leading to the bathroom. She had and elegant soul food dinner prepared, the table set and wine chilling on ice in the ice bucket. Everything was planned perfectly, even down to her showing up to Andre's family function, telling everyone that he said that he was coming later because he had some things to finish up at the office which is why they drove separate cars. See, Andre had a specially made car that allowed him to drive so that he would not have to depend upon others or inconvenience them. Even some of Rasheedah's own family and friends, who were also in attendance at Andre's family function and they too thought that Rasheedah's story seemed a little suspicious because Andre would never be a no show or late to one of his own family functions and even if he was late or going to be late he would call someone and let them know that he was going to be late and tell them where he was just in case something did happen. Andre never showed.

A neighbor, knowing that Andre was going to a family function, began getting worried because he and his family were also invited to the function and were riding with Andre. The neighbor noticed that Andre's car was still in the driveway and that it had not moved since Andre had come home from the office. The only reason why this neighbor took special notice on this particular night was because Andre had called him earlier and told him that he had a very strange feeling that he would not make it to the family function. It was like he had a premonition. Andre disappeared and was never seen or heard of again.

Being an attorney, Andre decided to get insurance on himself and their children. He and Rasheedah had four children, three boys and one girl. Two of the children were in their early to mid-twenties and only the sixteen- and eighteen-year-old remained at home. Being teens, they were often gone. After the first accident, Andre began documenting everything concerning the abusive relationship that he and Rasheedah had over the course of the years and how it had become even more intense once the children were just about grown or were grown. Andre left this information with this neighbor, family, and close family friends those that Andre could trust. He mentioned to them in the letters that in the event of his death, they were to open the envelope which would have instructions on what should be done. He changed his will using an out of state attorney who practiced law in several different states so that Rasheedah would not find out about the changing nor would any other lawyers that were directly associated to the two of them would know either.

This neighbor also had his own surveillance cameras. This longtime neighbor and friend to Andre called one of his friends to come over and decided to walk across the street to check on his friend Andre. He also knew that Rasheedah had been gone all night and had never come back from wherever she had gone. Through the window this neighbor and friend could see Andre's lifeless body laying on the floor and called the police. The police contacted the police in the state that Rasheedah was in and informed the family of Andre's death and had her picked up immediately as a person of interest. Rasheedah being the snake, manipulator, and high profiled lawyer that she was, she was able to get herself out of a pickle. The neighbors' surveillance cameras did not catch the perpetrators enter or leave Andre's house and the time of death which was long after Rasheedah had left the premises. The police were at a dead end and with the wires being cut to Andre's own surveillance cameras, fuses had been tampered with and the backup system not immediately kicking in the police had nothing further to go on. Andre's case had now become a cold case.

In Rasheedah's letter to the media, she admits that Andre's abuse by her was severe which is what lead up to his death. She also admitted that she was jealous because Andre was more obsessed with the job and spending time with his children and family than he was with her. She went on to say that Andre was becoming more successful and how she was not included in his plans and how he was beginning to dabble with politics advocating for disabled victims of domestic violence. Included in the letter Rasheedah explains that her abuse towards Andre was like taking a sledgehammer and beating him with it because at the time he was non-ambulatory (unable to walk without assistance being primarily confined to his wheelchair). Rasheedah also talked about how oftentimes, while in his wheelchair, Andre needed assistance being transferred from his wheelchair to a chair or to the bed, and how she would become frustrated and abused him. When these instances occurred, all it did would make situations worse because he would need even more assistance after she finished abusing him. The abuse had gotten so bad where Andre learned how to transfer himself from his wheelchair and anywhere else that he needed to be, in order to prevent the abuse from happening. What many could not understand is why was Rasheedah confessing now after 7 years? It was not just the fact that she felt guilty, it was the fact that she had an ulterior motive, another plan, one that no one knew about.

One of the reasons for Rasheedah abusing Andre was so that she could have power and control over him. Rasheedah did things such as telling Andre that their vows said until death did them part, she would use social isolation going with him to friends and family houses, she tried controlling his finances, not realizing that about five years into the marriage that he had gotten another bank account in a fictious name. She used intimidation, physical and sexual abuse, and she even neglected their children. Andre was well aware of this because Rasheedah did this out of spite. It was as though she had come to a point where she just hated Andre because everyone loved him, his personality, and his bubbly spirit. He was well respected and very charismatic despite the obstacles that he faced. He had the same uplifting spirit even after his last accident. He never allowed anyone to dull his shine and attention was always brought to him from a positive perspective.

Andre was not perfect, and he knew this, and yes of course he did have some enemies but not to the point where they wanted to cause him hurt, harm or danger. Rasheedah came from nothing, and Andre made her into something, making her independent having her own, but she wanted more, she wanted to splurge his money on shopping instead of buying his medications and the things that he needed in order for him to improve being on the road to recovery. She was so focused on her me syndrome that Andre and his sisters and cousins bought the children their clothes and what they needed. Rasheedah hindered Andre's progress during his recovery and this too Andre recognized. Every time, Andre recognized that something was not right, he quietly took matters into his own hands. When he was at the office, he had a personal trainer to come so that he could begin training again, and he would have the therapist and the nurse to come there as well, and without Rasheedah knowing it since she was now on another floor. And those who knew, never told, and lent a hand at helping him to get better.

In her book, under their fictious names, Rasheedah said that her and Andre were once high school sweethearts, but she got married right out of high school to one of the football players who had later been drafted by the NFL. Her abuse had begun with him. Her first husband left one summer going to training camp and never came back. The next thing she knew she received divorce papers, from the same deputies that were also evicting her from their home as her now ex-husband had put the house up for sell. This left Rasheedah in a precarious situation and very bitter causing her to have to move back in with her mother. One day while out, she decided to go by her old home and confront her ex only to find that the house had been sold. Becoming even more enraged, she drove back to her mother's house. Her mother handed her a certified envelope. Inside was a certified money order for a million dollars. This was from the sale of the house giving as her ex had given her half the money, even though it was in his name and he owned it before he married her, and a little more to just walk away and leave him alone. She never saw or heard from him again.

Rasheedah was 25 when she married Andre who was already established. Although they had once been high school sweethearts, they had not seen each other since they graduated. One day while in town, Andre happened to meet Rasheedah at a mom's and pop's restaurant. Haven blown through the money that her ex had given her, Andre provided Rasheedah with a job as a receptionist in the law firm. She then worked her way up. He sent her to school to be a paralegal and then she eventually went to law school, graduated, and passed the State Bar Exam. They eventually had four children two were now grown and out on their own, and the last two were 14 and 16. Rasheedah's abusive behavior had been going on since before high school towards others but became worse once the first two children had moved out. Rasheedah's abusive behavior was a learned behavior of seeing her mother abuse her father in front of her and her siblings with her being the youngest child. Rasheedah felt as though she was a bad seed since her mother had been married four times with three of the four husbands ending up dead under suspicious circumstances. Rasheedah's moms third husband chose to just leave paying off her mom a very generous amount and promising that he would never go to the police. The fourth husband wasn't as fortunate, but the third husband never said a thing until he found out about the eventual arrest and conviction of Rasheedah's mom who eventually took her own life while in prison, as the story goes. The only reason why Rasheedah's mom's third husband was not arrested for conspiracy to commit murder is because he had originally hired an attorney to file for a divorce and when he presented Lynne, Rasheedah's mom with the divorce papers she threatened to have her three brothers and her current boyfriend to kill him like they did her three husbands.

Rasheedah went on to say in her letter that 15 years before while expecting with their child, she had originally called the police lying and telling them that Andre had been abusing her knowing that he could be arrested and lose everything that he had worked for. The only problem with that story is that, with her being pregnant at the time, there were five of Andre's friends at the house that day and they all told the police that Rasheedah had been drinking and using drugs and Andre was trying to get her to stop drinking and using drugs telling her that it was not good for the baby. In addition, Andre was already a popular and well know attorney, so everyone knew his reputation and was familiar of what side of the tracks Rasheedah had come from. This was the first time that Rasheedah had went to Andre's safe where he kept his service gun since he had been in the military and was a sheriff's deputy before his accident of falling down those stairs at his friends' house. Rasheedah had been lying for years about her and Andre being high school sweethearts as Andre was 16 years older than Rasheedah. He was already established and had finished law school passing the bar. This is another reason why Rasheedah was so bitter because Andre was a handsome gentleman that kept himself in good shape and ate pretty healthy, and there were plenty women who were attracted to him. So, no matter what the situation, Andre knew that he would be able to defend himself.

In Rasheedah's book, she even wrote that she was not wise enough to wait for the police to leave the premises, she and began shooting wildly inside of the house. Her story changed often, as she forgot that she mentions that after the shooting incident inside of the house and her telling the police that she was cleaning the gun and running off at the mouth when it went off added more charges against her during the investigation. She went on to say that some neighbors, not realizing that the police were already at the premises called the police. Rasheedah had not known at the time that Andre had called one of the neighbors and he heard Rasheedah tell him that the only way that Andre would leave her was over his dead body in a body bag.

After that incident, Andre told Rasheedah to leave so that she would not be arrested since she had opened fire inside a residential dwelling endangering minors. He gave her money to get a room for a couple of nights. The police picked up Rasheedah before she was able to leave the yard arresting her anyway. Since Andre did not want to press charges against the mother of his children and being reminded of the fact that she was expecting that no charges be filed, there were no charges filed. Andre even refused to get a restraining order against Rasheedah, nor would Andre listen to his family, friends or coworker in obtaining one. Once their last baby was born and Andre thought that everything was okay, "the honeymoon period," one of Andre's children from his first marriage called to say that she was graduating from college and was inviting him and his new family to the graduation festivities. Rasheedah became enraged because of Andre's strong bond and relationship with his children, including the children that they had together and again she went for a weapon.

During another incident, Andre knew that with all of the loud noise, hollering and the throwing of items that the neighbors would again call the police. And again,

Andre told Rasheedah to leave before the police arrived. Once Rasheedah thought that the coast was clear and that the police was nowhere around, she came back to the house, went around to the back where Andre kept the weights that he used for working out and threw one of the 25-pound weights through the patio window shattering it sounding off the alarm. In a fit of rage, Rasheedah forgot about the surveillance cameras, so she had decided that she would go back to the house to make up with Andre only to find the house empty. Rasheedah did not know that Andre had taken the children and had gone to spend the rest of the weekend at his sister's house. Andre chosen this particular sister's home because Rasheedah did not know where she lived. This sister of Andre's never liked Rasheedah and had warned him against marrying her because she was evil and manipulative and had been since grammar school. Andre's sister always said that Rasheedah, the evil woman would be the death of him or one of those kids. So, at the request of his sister, Andre never told Rasheedah where his sister lived for safety reasons. After Andre's death, his sister said that she now regrets letting those words come out of her mouth. Proverbs 18:21, "Death and life are in the power of the tongue, and they that love it shall eat the fruit thereof."

Rasheedah's letter went on to say that she was glad that she changed her mind about accusing Andre of abusing her because he would have lost his job, and they would have been entangled in the judicial system and she would not have had the opportunity to benefit from his retirement or the income that he had from his other businesses or the property that he owned. It appeared that all Rasheedah was interested in were the dollar signs. Even though Rasheedah continued the violent behavior after all of the accusation, she was in denial refusing to recognize that she had a problem and needed help. As a matter of fact, this was Rasheedah's third marriage as she began that marriage with abuse once they were married, abusing that husband worse that she had Andre. That marriage lasted less than six months.

Now bitter because she had not benefitted from any of Andre's profits as he had changed his will without her knowing of it. She had gone so far to threaten the attorney's life that changed the will. This attorney did not play and told Rasheedah as much and let her know that he did not play with fire and was associated with some very powerful individual's such as those in the mafia and that she did not want to tangle with him. He also informed her that he knew of the great lengths that she had gone to, paying people to be a part of her scheme and promising others payment out of the insurance payments from Andre's death once she cashed in his policies. Dumbfounded, Rasheedah was not sure if this attorney that Andre had hired was bluffing or not, but she did not take any chances in getting tangled up with the mafia, and she, being familiar with the RICO statute, let that go.

Rasheedah also put in her letter that if her new husband tried to defend himself then she would threaten him by telling him that her uncles and a couple of her friends would take care of him and that there would be no trace of his body found. She also let him know that she would get away with it too as she was the widow of a former deputy and high-profile attorney and had gotten away with his murder. She went on to say that she had several acquaintances and associated who would believe that Andre abused her instead of her abusing him. The problem with Rasheedah and her stories is that she fabricated many of them. Her lines blurred between reality and make believe. Those in mental health stated that they were dealing with an individual who was a narcissist, and had psychosis, schizophrenia, and bipolar disorder.

In Rasheedah's letter, she mentioned that one day after only a few months of marriage to her second husband, she had come home from hanging out with friends and shopping only to find that he had packed his belongings and blew like the wind. Luckily, Rasheedah did not have the opportunity to get to know any of his family and friends as she had forbidden him not to have contact with anyone from his past. Rumor had it that he moved back to New York never to have contact with her again.

Again, being very bitter and enraged, Rasheedah began taking her abuse out on the people that worked for her. She had already been aggressive towards them, but because of their loyalty to Andre many stayed, and even those who originally stayed were beginning to leave when situations were too much to bear. Rasheedah's life as she knew it was beginning to fall apart, she knew that Andre would never tell anyone of his ordeal at home because he did not want to be shunned by other guys or anyone else, because they would view him as being weak. He was a former peace officer later he became an officer of the court, and he knew how being abused by his wife would that look. Again, Rasheedah did not know just how many people Andre talked to about his situation months before his death, nor did she know how much evidence that he had been collecting for year, nor did she know just how many people had copies of this evidence.

Rasheedah continued her letter about how her and Andre would to restaurants, clubs, or other outings and once she began drinking, she would first become verbally abusive, then that verbal abuse would become physical. Those who were closest to them such as family and friends knew of her abusive behaviors and would try to talk her into getting some help. That would not help calm the situation as she would go off on them, wither verbally or physically. There were those who would just tolerate her behavior waiting for it to eventually pass, while others shunned away only to stay close to Andre in private as not to put him or the kids in further jeopardy. Rasheedah had gotten so abusive to a point where people would invite Andre and the children to outings but not her. This confused and frustrated Rasheedah because she couldn't understand why everyone was keeping their distance from her including her family, and Andre's family did not care much for her, so their being distance was not surprising. Once their older children became adults, up until Andre's death, their own children limited their visits with their parents and younger siblings because of their mom's abusive behaviors.

Once Andre passed away, the younger children felt that it was best that they moved in with their older siblings and just stop visiting their mom at all because they knew deep down in their hearts that their mother was the actual cause of their father's death but could not do anything about it because of the control that their mother had over certain people. Again, Rasheedah did not realize that Andre had left his own children, the ones from his first marriage along with family from both sides and friends the evidence that he had been accumulating over the years.

Shortly after Rasheedah had sent her letter and a copy of the book to the media, she had been bragging and boasting about how she wrote a book and actually got away with murder with the help of her brothers, her exes, and known acquaintances that she once represented. She had become the epitome of her own demise. Remember, that life and death are in the power of the tongue. Rasheedah never went to church and hadn't thought much about religion, but Andre was an advent church goer and a deacon in the church and took his children with him faithfully, even after his accident.

One of Rasheedah's sisters bought a copy of her sister's books as recommended by a family friend as she too kept her distance from her sister. She then contacted

Andre's sister who never cared for Rasheedah as she knew where the sister lived but never told her own sister. The sister-in-law's then contacted nieces and nephews gave copies of all of the evidence that they had been collecting over the years to their attorney's, in addition to giving copies to the media. This was the beginning of the end for Rasheedah as she knew it as her world was getting ready to crumble around her.

One thing that Rasheedah failed to realize is that when family and friends would visit Andre and the children and take them on outings, Andre recorded and then had the recordings transcribed demonstrating his versions of the abuse. Since Rasheedah refused to give Andre a divorce, this is when Andre decided that he would give copies of everything that he had complied against her to an out of state attorney informing him that in the event of his death, the information was to be released. Someone decided to give the police a copy of what they had in hopes that they could do an investigation to intervene and protect Andre and the two children who were living at home. The sad part is that the police were aware of this evidence and decided to sit on it telling this anonymous person that there was nothing that could be done unless there was an attempt on Andre's life. It was only when Rasheedah had published her book and wrote those letters to the media did, they decide to take action and hand the evidence over to the district attorney's office. The good this is that the anonymous person who had provided the police department with copies of the information that Andre had given them, they also provided the district attorney and the FBI with this same information as they did not trust the police. Even the police department did not know that they were being investigated by the FBI along with Rasheedah. Because of the police department's lack of concern to look into the matter with Andre and Rasheedah based on evidence given to them, they and the city were eventually sued by Andre's family and his children for not only waiting so long to provide the family with justice but for allowing others to be put in the way of harm, hurt and danger. They had not even bothered to contact the department of children's social services to at least protect the children.

The problem with this society today is that worldwide, this society has this stereotypical, gender biased and discriminative attitude against men that women who are batterers of men rarely exist and are limited to none. This is the type of attitude is displayed because those in the political, judicial and media realm refuse to recognize that such problems do exists. These men then become vulnerable to such abuses by wives, exes and girlfriends because of the fear of public backlash, or they have a fear of being arrested and thrown into a faulty judicial system, being falsely accused of crimes that they did not commit, the loss of their children, everything that they have worked for and the loss of their dignity.

The reason why such information is suppressed is again because of advocates who focus only on females who are abused by men. The media will put a spin on the situation leaving doubt in the public's mind, "well what did he do to make her so mad?" There are also certain political influences that are given to feministic powers which demonstrates that there are only certain advocates who will convey to the world that such feministic powers can abuse their power. Just like there are men who stand up for women's rights that abuse is wrong, there should also be women who should stand up for men who are also being abused by other women. Two wrongs don't make it right and domestic abuse and violence against anyone is wrong. This is an issue that must be recognized, nipped in the bud, taken more seriously and stopped.

References

Black, M.C., Basile, K.C., Breiding, M.J., Smith, S.G., Walters, M.L., Merrick, M.T., Chen, J., & Stevens, M.R. (2011). The National Intimate Partner and Sexual Violence Survey (NISVS): 2010 Summary Report. Atlanta, GA: National Center for Injury Prevention and Control, Centers for Disease Control and Prevention. Available at: http://www.cdc.gov/ViolencePrevention/pdf/NISVS_Report2010-a.pdf

Catalano, S. (2005). Intimate partner violence in the United States 1993-2005. U.S. Bureau of Justice Statistics. Retrieved from: http://bjs.ojp.usdoj.gov/content/intimate/table/vomen.cfm National Crime Victimization Survey data.

Cook, P. W. (2009). Abused men: The hidden side of domestic violence (2nd ed.). Westport: Praeger.

Douglas, E.M. and Hines, D. (2011) "The help seeking experiences of men who sustain intimate partner violence: An overlooked population and implications for practice." J. Fam. Vio. 2011 Aug;26(6):473-485 Published online 04 June 2011. National Institute of Mental Health Grant Number 5R21MH074590. Available at: http://www.clarku.edu/faculty/dhines/Douglas%20%20Hines%202011%20helpseekin g%20experiences%20of%20male%20victims.pdf

Galdas, P. M., Cheater, F., & Marshall, P. (2005). Men and health help seeking behavior: literature review. Journal of Advanced Nursing, 49(6), 616-622

Hines, D. A., Brown, J., & Dunning, E. (2007). Characteristics of callers to the domestic abuse helpline for men. Journal of Family Violence, 22(2), 63-72. Available at: http://www.clarku.edu/faculty/dhines/Hines%20Brown%20and%20Dunning%202007 %20DAHM.pdf

Hoff, B. H. (2001), The Risk of Serious Physical Injury from Assault by a Woman Intimate: A Re-Examination of National Violence Against Women Survey Data on Type of Assault by an Intimate. Men Web On-line Journal (ISSN: 1095-5240 http://www.menweb.org/NVAWSrisk.htm) Retrieved from Web on Jan. 18, 2011.

Saltzman LE, Fanslow JL, McMahon PM, Shelley GA. Intimate Partner Violence Surveillance: Uniform definitions and recommended data elements, Version 1.0. Atlanta

(GA): National Center for Injury Prevention and Control, Centers for Disease Control and Prevention; 1999. This is the most current version of this document, as of January 19, 2011.

Statistics Canada (2011 January). Family Violence in Canada: A Statistical Profile Catalogue no. 85-224-X, pp. 7-8. Retrieved from http://www.statcan.gc.ca/pub/85-224x/85-224-x2010000-eng.pdf

Statistics Canada (2006, October). Measuring violence against women: Statistical trends 2006 (Catalogue No. 85-570-XIE). Ottawa, ON: Author. Retrieved from http://www.statcan.ca/english/research/85-570-XIE/85-570-XIE2006001.pdf (654,000 women and 546,000 men – men 45.5%)

Straus, M.A. (2011). Gender symmetry and mutuality in perpetration of clinical-level partner violence: Empirical evidence and implications for prevention and treatment. Aggression and Violent Behavior 16 (2011) 279-288. Available at: http://pubpages.unh.edu/~mas2/V78%20Clincal%20level%20symmetry-Published-11.pdf

Straus, M. A. (2005). Women's violence toward men is a serious social problem. In D.R. Loseke, R. J. Gelles & M. M. Cavanaugh (Eds.), Current controversies on family violence, 2nd Edition (2nd Edition ed., pp. 55-77). Newbury Park: Sage Publications. Available at: http://pubpages.unh.edu/~mas2/VB33R%20Women's%20Violence%20Toward%20Men.pdf

Straus, M. A. (1995). Trends in cultural norms and rates of partner violence: an update to 1992. In S. Stith & M. A. Straus (Eds.), Understanding partner violence: Prevalence, causes, consequences, and solutions (pp. 30-33). Minneapolis: National Council on Family Relations. Available at: http://pubpages.unh.edu/~mas2/V56.pdf

Straus, M. A., & Gelles, R. J. (1988). How violent are American families? Estimates from the National Family Violence Resurvey and other studies. In G. T. Hotaling & D. Finkelhor (Eds.), Family abuse and its consequences: New directions in research (pp. 14-36). Thousand Oaks: Sage Publications.

Tjaden, P. G., & Thoennes, N. (2000). Full Report of Prevalence, Incidence and Consequences of Violence Against Women: Findings from the National Violence Against Women Survey. U.S. Department of Justice, National Institute of Justice & Centers for

Disease Control and Prevention Research Report, Nov. 2000. NCJ 183781

Truman, J.S., (2011). National Crime Victimization Survey: Criminal Victimization, 2010. U.S. Department of Justice, Office of Justice Programs, Bureau of Justice Statistics. NCJ 235508

U.S. Department of Justice, Office of Justice Programs, National Institute of Justice (2005, Nov.). Solicitation for Proposals: Justice Responses to Intimate Partner Violence and Stalking. Catalog of Federal Domestic Assistance (CFDA) Number: 16.560 CFDA Title: National Institute of Justice Research, Evaluation, and Development Project. Grants Grants.gov Funding No. 2006-NIJ-1207 SL 000734. The 2007 solicitation, Intimate Partner Violence and Stalking: Research for Policy and Practice, CFDA No. 16.560, the last year of the research for policy and practice funding, states: "Within these priority areas, applicants may submit proposals that examine the criminal justice response to intimate partner violence and/or stalking as it occurs within diverse populations. This might include, but is not limited to, studies that focus on ethnic, racial, and language minority groups including immigrants; Native American women; women who live in rural areas; women with cognitive, developmental, or physical disabilities; women with vision impairments; elderly women; women living in institutional settings; women who are migrant workers; women involved in prostitution; and homeless women." (p. 5)

Woods v. Horton (2008), 167 Cal.App.4th 658 CA Ct. of Appeal 3rd Dist. 08 C.D.O.S. 13247 "We find the gender-based classifications in the challenged statutes that provide programs for victims of domestic violence violate equal protection. We find male victims of domestic violence are similarly situated to female victims for purposes of the statutory programs and no compelling state interest justifies the gender classification. We reform the affected statutes by invalidating the exemption of males and extending the statutory benefits to men, whom the Legislature improperly excluded." See Men & Women Against Discrimination v. The Family Protection Services Bd., Kanawa County (VWA) Circuit Court, Civil Cause No. 08-C-1056. Decision filed Oct. 2, 2009.

Source: http://batteredmen.com/NISVS.htm

By eb|February 12th, 2012|Research, Uncategorized Comments Off on CDC Study: More Men than Women Victims of Partner Abuse

Sources:

[1] "Violence against Women." WHO. Nov. 2014. Web. 24 June 2015.

[2] WHO United Nations, London School of Hygiene & Tropical Medicine, South African Medical Research Council. Department of Reproductive Health and Research. *Global and Regional Estimates of Violence against Women: Prevalence and Health Effects of Intimate Partner Violence and Non-Partner Sexual Violence.* World Health Organization, 2013.

[3] USA. U.S. Department of Justice. Office of Justice Programs, Bureau of Justice Statistics. *Homicide Trends in the United States, 1980-2008.* By Alexia Cooper and Erica L. Smith. Office of Justice Programs, 2011. NCJ 236018.

[4] USA. California Department of Justice. Division of California Justice Information Services, Bureau of Criminal Information and Analysis, Criminal Justice Statistics Center. *Homicide in California 2013.* Comp. Kamala D. Harris. California Department of Justice, 2013.

[5] "Violence against Women." *WHO.* World Health Organization, Nov. 2014. Web. 24 June 2015.

[6] USA. U.S. Department of Justice. Office of Justice Programs, Bureau of Justice Statistics. *Nonfatal Domestic Violence, 2003–2012.* By Jennifer L. Truman and Rachel E. Morgan. Office of Justice Programs, 2014. NCJ244697.

[7] United Nations. Secretary-General Campaigns. *Unite to End Violence Against Women Factsheet.* United Nations Department of Public Information, 2008.

[8] Munson, Michael. *Sheltering Transgender Women: Providing Welcoming Services.* Forge, National Resource Center on Domestic Violence, 2014.

[9] Walters, Mikel L., Jieru Chen, and Matthew J. Breiding. *The National Intimate Partner and Sexual Violence Survey (NISVS): 2010 Findings on Victimization by Sexual Orientation.* Rep. Atlanta: National Center for Injury Prevention and Control Centers for Disease Control and Prevention, 2013.

[10] Wahab, Stéphanie, Ph.D., and Lenora Olson, M.A. *Intimate Partner Violence and Sexual Assault in Native American Communities.* Rep. no. 353-366. 4th ed. Vol. 5. Sage Publications, 2004. Trauma, Violence, & Abuse.

[11] "Dating Abuse Statistics – Www.loveisrespect.org." *www.loveisrespect.org.* Love Is Respect, Web. 24 June 2015.

[12] "Intimate Partner Violence during Pregnancy: A Guide for Clinicians." *Centers for Disease Control and Prevention*. Centers for Disease Control and Prevention. Web. 24 June 2015.

[13] World Health Organization, Pan Health Organization. *Intimate Partner Violence: Understanding and Addressing Violence against Women*. RHR ed. Ser. 12.36. World Health Organization, Pan Health Organization, 2012.

[14] "Domestic Violence Statistics." *American Bar Association Commission on Domestic and Sexual Violence*. Web. 24 June 2015.

[15] Brown, Brené. *I Thought It Was Just Me (but It Isn't): Making the Journey from "what Will People Think?" to "I Am Enough"* New York: Gotham, 2008. Print.

[16] *Domestic Violence and Homelessness Factsheet*. American Civil Liberties Union, 2008.

[17] *A Framework for Understanding: The Nature and Dynamics of Domestic Violence*. The Missouri Coalition Against Domestic Violence, March 2005.)

[18] Bennett, Larry, and Oliver Williams. "Controversies and Recent Studies of Batterer Intervention Program Effectiveness." *VAWAnet.org*. National Resource Center on Domestic Violence, 2011. Web.

[19] Herman-Lewis, Judit. *Trauma and Recovery: The Aftermath of Violence-from Domestic Abuse to Political Terror*. New York: Basic, 1992. Print.

[20]Ferencik, Sonia D., and Rachel Ramirez-Hammond. *Trauma-informed Care Best Practices and Protocols for Ohio's Domestic Violence Programs*. Publication. Ohio Domestic Violence Network, 2011.

Sources: Paul Elam is Editor-in-Chief for Men's News Daily and the publisher of A Voice for Men.

CDC Report www.cdc.gov/ncipc/dvp/ipv_factsheet.pdf
NIJ Report www.ncjrs.gov/App/Publications/abstract.aspx?ID=199709 Las Vegas Sun

1. National Family Violence Legislative Resource Center:

When we ignore male victims of domestic abuse, we also ignore their children, who continue to be damaged by witnessing the violence regardless of how severe it is. We cannot break this intergenerational cycle by ignoring half of it. That's why a global coalition of experts has formed to support a research-based, inclusive approach, and their website has solid data showing women initiate the violence as often as men.

2. Men are More Likely Than Women to Be Victims in Dating Violence:

A recent 32-nation study by the University of New Hampshire found female students initiate partner violence as often as male students and controlling behavior exists equally in perpetrators of both sexes.

3. Women More Likely to be Perpetrators of Abuse as Well as Victims:

A University of Florida study recently found women are more likely than men to "stalk, attack and abuse" their partners.

"We're seeing women in relationships acting differently nowadays than we have in the past," said Angela Gover, a UF criminologist who led the research. "The nature of criminality has been changing for females, and this change is reflected in intimate relationships as well."

4. Teenage Violence Linked to Later Domestic Violence:

A University of Washington study recently found women were nearly twice as likely as men to perpetrate domestic violence in the past year including kicking, biting or punching their partner, threatening to hit or throw something at their partner, and pushing, grabbing or shoving their partner.

5. Assaults by Women on Their Spouses or Male Partners:

Virtually all sociological data shows women initiate domestic violence as often as men, that women use weapons more than men, and that 38% of injured victims are men. California State University Professor Martin Fiebert summarizes almost 200 of these studies online.

6. Journal of Family Violence:

A recent study in the Journal of Family Violence found many male callers to a national hotline experienced high rates of severe violence from female partners who used violence to control them.

7. Intimate Partner Abuse Against Men:

Some scholars suggest that the motives for intimate partner abuse against men by women may differ from those for abuse against women by men, and that women suffer more severe injuries than men. Nonetheless, the occurrence of abuse by women against men, and its consequences, warrant attention. It is important for the victims of abuse, whether they be men or women, to know that they are not alone – that is, that such experience is not unique to their personal situation.

It is also important for the perpetrators of intimate partner abuse – men or women – to recognize that violence in any form is both morally and legally wrong.

8. Disabusing the Definition of Domestic Abuse:

A law review article by law Professor Linda Kelly that documents the long history of how battered men's statistics and plight have been intentionally covered up.

9. Transforming a Flawed Policy:

This is a cutting-edge challenge to the domestic violence industry by Professor Don Dutton, a domestic violence expert who was a prosecutorial witness in the O.J. Simpson case and who challenges the man bad/woman good model and the notion that women mostly hit in self-defense.

10. Why Women Assault:

California State University surveyed 1,000 college women: 30% admitted they assaulted a male partner.

Their most common reasons: (1) my partner wasn't listening to me; (2) my partner wasn't being sensitive to my needs; and (3) I wished to gain my partner's attention.

For more information see:

A University of Pennsylvania emergency room report found 13% of men reported being assaulted by a female partner in the previous 12 months, of which 50% were choked, kicked, bitten, punched, or had an object thrown at them, 37% involved a weapon, and 14% required medical attention, at **Academic of Emergency Medicine**

University of Pennsylvania Professor Richard Gelles states: "Contrary to the claim that women only hit in self-defense, we found that women were as likely to initiate the violence as were men. In order to correct for a possible bias in reporting, we reexamined our data looking only at the self-reports of women. The women reported similar rates of female-to-male violence compared to male-to-female, and women also reported they were as likely to initiate the violence as were men," in his article reprinted at **The Hidden Side of Domestic Violence**
Help for men

Unlike the United States, the police services in the United Kingdom has several locations that they have expanded with regard to their domestic violence programs and the way in which they respond in efforts to deal with IPV against men. There are also shelters that have been specifically designed for males of domestic violence as they begin their healing process; as of 2010, there were "sixty refuge places available to men throughout England and Wales, compared to 7,500 places for women."[191]

[191] Campbell, Denis (September 5, 2010). *"More than 40% of domestic violence victims are male, report reveals"*. *The Guardian.*

Made in the USA
Columbia, SC
31 July 2023

20925277R10068